MAKE IT DO

A Spitfire Pilot's True Story of World War 2 Grit and Survival

Ken Cam

Copyright © 2025 by Peter Cam

All rights reserved.

No part of this book may be reproduced in any form or by any electronic or mechanical means, including information storage and retrieval systems, without written permission from the copyright holder, except for the use of brief quotations in a book review.

For Publishing/Editorial enquiries, please contact:

michael@published-authority.com

Here's the book at long last,
packed with stories of the past.
None are fiction, all are true,
and now they're written down for you.
Do turn the pages and read the rest,
and just remember —
"I did my best."

— Dad

Contents

Four Weeks	vii
Preface	ix
1. Opening Sortie	1
2. Childhood	4
3. The Rumblings of War	8
4. Call-up	12
5. Induction	15
6. Aircrew Ground School	19
7. Elementary Flying Training School	23
8. Service Flying Training School	27
9. Operational Training Unit	33
10. The First Fighter Squadron	36
11. Operations	44
12. More of the Same Thing	50
13. Cornwall	55
14. Diversions From the Norm	59
15. Embarkation and Disembarkation	69
16. The Campaign Called "Torch"	76
17. The Festive Season 1942	83
18. The Campaign Continues	89
19. The Final Stages of "Torch"	93
20. A Change is as Good as a Rest	100
21. The Boat Trip	108
22. A Life Under the Ocean Waves	113
23. Mainland Italy	118
24. Train Journey Number One	122
25. Solitary Confinement	125
26. My New Life	129
27. On the Move Again	133
28. Moosburg - Fort Bismark - Weinburg - Sagan	137
29. Stalag Luft III - Sagan	142
30. The Year of 1944	150
31. On the Move Again	159
32. Rest and be Thankful	164

33. Liberation	168
34. Homeward Bound	174
35. Home at Last	178
36. Rehabilitation and the RAF	181
37. On the Move - Yet Again	187
38. Palestinian Incidents	192
39. A Commendation - A Black Mark - and A Claim to Fame	203
40. The Journey Homewards	209
41. Closing Sortie	214
The Post-War Life of Ken Cam	217

Four Weeks

When Ken Cam joined the Royal Air Force, the average life expectancy of a Spitfire pilot was just four weeks.

Ken flew for more than four years.

This is his story.

Preface

I am sticking my neck out here because I do not know the technical difference between an introduction and a preface or, for that matter, a foreword. I was initially asked by my sons, David and Peter, to write about my war stories, but I have expanded that to include my childhood, the onset of war, and my departure from the safe surroundings of home, as well as some post-war memories.

As far as the pages about war are concerned, and having read other authors (if I may call myself an author), I have found within them writings that would have, at the time of the stories, been called "Line Shooting"[*] by many of my squadron compatriots. This Line Shooting may have gone down well with our American friends, but I feel it is not truly British, as they say, and so I have tried hard to avoid the trap.

The opinions I have quoted are mine, rightly or wrongly, and the facts related are as truthful as memory allows. I sincerely hope that you will find the words within these pages interesting reading.

Betty, Mum, or Granny (whichever is relevant to you) generously offered to type the whole manuscript. The whole project is, therefore, a

---

[*] In British military slang, "line shooting" refers to exaggerating stories, bragging, or telling self-glorifying tales about one's wartime experiences.

Preface

communal effort. It was commenced in the late Summer of 1997, precisely fifty years after I left the Royal Air Force in October 1947.

So now, David and Peter read on, and remember, you asked for it!

Ken Cam
Lancashire
July 1999

Chapter 1

Opening Sortie

We crossed the coast, and I saw that the Commanding Officer had chosen a course that was all but due east. It was going to be another beautiful day. Since this flight was at a very low level (to avoid German radar operating from Sicily), it was unlikely that we would encounter any opposition. I was looking forward to a peaceful flight for a change. Quite suddenly, I saw a small puff of white exhaust smoke come from one of the exhaust stubs. Surely not, I thought. I knew precisely what white smoke indicated; it meant the mechanical failure of the engine, and I waited with very bated breath for another sign. There was nothing for a minute or two, and then, to my horror, another puff and another, and eventually a steady stream. I looked at the radiator temperature gauge; it was climbing.

I opened the radiator flap to allow more cold air to circulate. This had no effect whatsoever. This was indeed trouble, and we were over the sea to add to the bargain. I switched to transmit: "Blue One" (or whatever my colour was at that time) "Blue One to Leader - Glycol Leak - Switching off." I had two options: ditch it in the sea or try to climb to a sufficient height, then bail out. The engine was still running, and although the ride was bumpy, it maintained flying speed. I decided to get some height, if possible. I didn't fancy ditching as a Spitfire would sink seven seconds after coming to rest on the sea. I immediately pulled the knob and jettisoned the hood, then pulled the radio plug out and removed my helmet, throwing it out. I was no longer in touch with the other aircraft.

Gently, I climbed, maintaining an easterly course. I managed around two thousand feet in fits and starts before the engine seized up, and the propeller came to rest. I knew all the procedures off by heart for the various escape methods. Turn the plane on its back and try to kick the stick forward as you get out. This helps to eject you from the cockpit. The dinghy is located between your bottom and the parachute, and just before you hit the sea, the parachute harness should be released. This automatically pulls the cover off the dinghy, and theoretically, it should land in the sea near you. There is a small bottle of compressed gas attached to the dinghy. You turn it on, and the dinghy inflates.

I started the routine, and as I turned the aircraft onto its back, I saw two little pimples of land protruding through a morning mist. I kept turning, brought the plane upright again, and inspected the new find. Yes - it was land of some sort, but what and where? Maps of the area were practically non-existent, and in any case, I certainly didn't have one. Anyway, I thought it was better to land one way or the other near land than in the middle of the sea. I put my straps back on and decided to take a look, hoping to crash the thing onto terra firma. This was a third option that, just a short time before, had not been considered at all. As I circled down, the rest of the squadron also circled once or twice, and when they saw what I was about to do, they turned east and went on their way. As I descended, I reached a height too low for parachuting, so I was now really committed.

Eventually, I saw that the land was, in fact, a tiny island with a couple of extinct volcanoes rising from it. I searched for a flat spot to land. The best and really the only place was a stretch on the east side of the island, so I made my preparations. I did some "S" bends to get my approach and height correct for the crash landing. I tightened the straps and pulled them repeatedly. On the final approach, I turned off the petrol and all switches and lowered the seat fully. I was approaching too fast, so I pulled back on the stick once or twice, but it didn't seem to make much difference. I was quickly running out of time, and as you will realise, a second attempt was impossible. In a few seconds, I mentally reviewed the procedure for a belly landing, and I had covered everything that needed to be done. Just before I touched down, I glanced at the airspeed indicator and realised I was travelling far too fast, but I could do nothing about it.

There was a loud crunch, and bits of the propeller flew off. I hit what seemed to be a sort of stone wall. Many years later, when I returned to the island and saw that there were no stone walls in that area, I knew I must have ploughed through a wall of cactus plants about three or four feet high. Nevertheless, the result was that it threw me into a cartwheel. This violent motion dislodged both wings, and I barreled on. After a few more obstacles, I somersaulted twice and lost the back half of the fuselage. I was conscious of all this happening, and finally, what was left of the Spitfire turned over and screwed its nose into a mound. At long last, I was motionless. There was no sound, no feeling, no sight. I literally thought I was dead.

Chapter 2
Childhood

It should be said from the outset that my childhood was a happy time, although strict and somewhat restricted by today's standards. I was born in Blackpool, England, on August 4, 1921, into a household comprising my father, mother, grandmother (on my mother's side), and my sister, Kathleen, who was then about two and a half years old. Although money was plentiful at the time, we children were severely restricted in our spending. However, this was not seen to be a problem, as we thoroughly enjoyed our allocation. I remember Kathleen and I used to go down to the bottom of King George Avenue and round the corner in Holmfield Road to visit a small sweet shop, clutching our weekly one penny. Occasionally, we would be rather rash and invest the whole amount on two ounces of sweets; otherwise, we would spend half of it on one ounce and return later in the week to spend our remaining half-penny. It was not considered desirable to assume, or even be guilty of, affluence — a lesson which has stayed with us. We were told many years later that, as children, we asked for nothing, which would suggest that the lesson of living within one's income had been truly learned and has stood us in good stead. We were short of nothing. I do not intend to be a moralist, but I am trying to recapture thoughts from childhood.

When I was four years old, I recall being on the receiving end of the "strap," a razor strap suitably cut at the end to resemble a cat-o'-nine-tails. I received a tricycle, which was an absolute delight. Bear in mind that in the 1920s, there was very little traffic, and one day during the early days of Blackpool Illuminations, I set off on an adventure and pedalled as far as the Pleasure Beach, along the Promenade (not the roadway), and was gone for hours. I remember weaving in and out of pedestrians. Meanwhile, the whole household was out searching, including the Police, and I believe my grandma was the one who spotted me on my return journey somewhere near the Manchester Hotel. I recall hiding under the kitchen table, cornered by Father, who had a somewhat stiff leg and could not quite reach me with the strap. Further punishment came in the form of being sent to bed, followed by the temporary withdrawal of the tricycle.

By this time, Kathleen had started school at a small private establishment called Langdale School on Argyle Road, and I was keen to join her. This request was honoured, and I started school shortly before I was five. My sister was the first pupil to pass her scholarship from that school—no mean feat!

Around this time, when I was between five and six years old, my father had a garage built at the end of our rather long back garden, and shortly after, a brand-new motorcar arrived. This was a 1927 Hillman 14-horsepower family saloon in maroon with cream-painted spoked wheels. Very roomy with flower vases and luxurious appointments. The original invoice is still around, and the cost was £400 on the road. Motor insurance was not mandatory at the time, and a driving licence cost five shillings (25 pence). Driving tests were, of course, non-existent. Our next-door neighbour, the Brierleys, had a chauffeur who was teaching Mother to drive. By now, my father had relinquished driving due, no doubt, to the onset of asthma and subsequent heart problems. We would venture in the car to places like Backbarrow, Malham Tarn in Yorkshire, Semerwater, North Wales via Llangollen, Lake Bala, Barmouth, and the like. Occasionally, we would encounter another vehicle, perhaps every half-hour or so.

Ken's dad, mum and sister sitting at the front of the Hillman saloon. Circa 1919

Holidays and picnics were now a frequent feature, but my father would never stay in a hotel - the reason unknown - so when we did stay somewhere on holidays, it was either with friends or at a recommended farm. The Trough of Bowland, Dunsop Bridge, Abbeystead, etc., were favourites. They were delightful times. On two occasions, I recall staying at a farm just outside Llangollen, and we made two abortive attempts to travel up Snowdon on the mountain railway - and I still have not made the trip to this day.

And so life progressed until 1932, when Father's health quickly deteriorated, and in June, he died. That particular day, Kathleen and I were sitting on deck chairs in the garage when I shot up and said, "Daddy is dead." How I knew, I do not know.

Kathleen and I were not allowed to attend the funeral. Sometime later, we moved house, and the car was sold. Kathleen, by then, was attending the Blackpool Collegiate School, and I was transferred to Claremont School, where I remained for a short time before changing to the grammar school. I began to really miss having Father, as living with three females, I felt as though I was starved of a man to answer my problems. Apart from this aspect, home life was good, and I have been a 'homebird' ever since.

MAKE IT DO

The next phase of my life had commenced.

Unlock Ken's Lost Chapters

Scan the QR code below to get **exclusive access** to three original chapters from Ken's memoir that didn't make the final print — plus a **full copy of the original manuscript, exactly as Ken wrote it**.
These bonus chapters include rare stories, bonus photography, and raw moments from Ken's time in service — preserved just for you.

Chapter 3

The Rumblings of War

The year 1939 brought with it rumblings of war in Europe. Herr Hitler was intent on being the master of Europe and continued to overrun neighbouring countries and absorb them into his domain. By July that year, he had successfully acquired a fair chunk, and his intentions were plain. This, of course, was unacceptable to those in power in the UK. Eventually, Mr. Chamberlain was dispatched to confront Hitler and demand a solemn declaration from him that his project for European domination would cease.

On Sunday, September 3, 1939, Mr Chamberlain announced to the country over the wireless at 11:00 a.m. that the United Kingdom was at war with Germany, as no declaration had been received from Hitler. This news was a shock to all, especially those of an age who had survived the Great War of 1914-1918. To us youths, the impression seemed to be that, in our ignorance, the whole affair would quickly disappear. At the same time, we expected German bombers to appear in the skies above at any time. Nevertheless, preparations for war were immediately put into hand. Those who had been members of the Territorial Army were immediately called up and proceeded to their respective units to begin intense training.

In hindsight, the country was ill-prepared for war, and the lack of equipment was astounding. Preparations to counter an invasion were initiated, and roadblocks were constructed at the entrances to towns, particularly those located near or on the coast. By year-end, these barricades and pillboxes required personnel to man them. To this end, an organisation called the Local Defence Volunteers (LDV) was formed. Apparently, I was keen to help and immediately joined the Blackpool branch of this LDV. Our headquarters were in the basement of the Town Hall in Talbot Square, and here we were issued armbands and a pickaxe handle. I don't recall how many nights per week we were on duty, but we slept in uncomfortable beds in the basement and had, I believe, two hours of duty and two hours off. Our job was to stop all vehicles at a particular barrier and demand to see the Identity Card of all persons aboard. I am sure that not many people were intimidated by a youth armed with a pickaxe handle, and we suffered some very rude remarks while trying our best to do our duty. Later on, we were issued with Great War Ross Rifles, which were even more cumbersome. We were, of course, not issued with any cartridges, but this was a secret!

Sometimes, during the long nights, we would go to an all-night cafe in Coronation Street, where, for two pennies, we could obtain a plate of what was called "Loose Stuff." This was the liquid remaining from a hot pot. Occasionally, one was lucky enough to get solid potatoes, onions, or even meat! Still, beggars cannot be choosers, so we did our best with a spoon and a thick slice of bread. Nevertheless, it was a pleasant and welcome diversion.

Preparations for all sorts were accelerated, and the permanent army and the Territorial Army were dispatched to France to counter Hitler's advance. I do not doubt at all that the British Expeditionary Force (BEF) did its utmost with minimal equipment, but it was no match for the now well-experienced and well-equipped German forces. The campaign ended in June 1940 with its collapse and the renowned withdrawal from Dunkirk. All manner of ships were used to cross the English Channel and retrieve as many men as possible. Needless to say, some of the forces were taken prisoners and were kept as such for five years until victory was achieved.

At the beginning of June 1940, I must have decided that my particular war effort in the LDV was not good enough and that I should offer my services to be trained to do a better job. My friend and I, therefore, went down to the Labour Exchange on Tyldesley Road. This had become a recruiting depot, and we decided that the Royal Air Force (RAF) was our choice. As volunteers, we had several options, such as joining the Army, Navy, or Air Force. We were both interested in things mechanical and filled out the application form accordingly. The fellow who accepted and read our forms noticed that we were both grammar school educated and immediately crossed out the word 'Mechanic' and substituted it with the words 'UT Pilot' and 'Air Observer' (UT meaning 'under training'). The prospect of this somewhat delighted us, although I still told my mother I had volunteered as a mechanic. It was some time later that I had to admit what I was really going to do. Within a few days, I had a letter and railway warrant to attend a Church Hall off Fishergate in Preston for a medical examination. This was merely, I think, to ensure that I possessed all the necessary limbs, eyes, ears, etc. It took about five minutes, and I returned home.

Very shortly after this, I received another letter and railway warrant to attend RAF Padgate, near Warrington. I was told I was to stay for a few days. This was for intensive medical and educational examinations. The medical lasted quite a few hours and was spread over a couple of days. Educational tests followed, and unfortunately, my friend failed his algebra or something and was told to reapply in six months. Having passed all the required tests, I joined the other successful applicants in a room for attestation.

This word was meaningless to me, but I soon came to understand it. Until now, we had been treated in a rather gentlemanly fashion, but upon leaving the room after swearing allegiance to the King and signing a form to that effect, we assembled outside. Then came the shattering introduction to the Corporal, who immediately used his loudest voice to assemble us to form a Squad. The gentlemanly bit was now a thing of the past, and we were shouted at and bellowed at until we reached the railway station for our return home. Signing the attestation paper shoved us into a vastly different world!

Whilst at Padgate, we heard a night bombing raid — our first — this was directed at Manchester or Liverpool, I forget which, but it was certainly a taste of things to come. The final act of the Corporal was to give us our railway warrant and say a crude farewell, reminding us all that we were now subject to Service Rules and Regulations and, of course, Military Discipline and that we had signed on until the end of the present emergency—whenever that would be. It all sounded very ominous, yet it was tinged with a certain amount of welcome, adventure, expectation, and not a little pride in that we were about to "do our bit for the country". How big or little a bit remained to be seen. A peaceful life was about to be exchanged for an altogether different sort.

We boarded our respective trains and headed home to await the next stage.

Ken, aged 18

Chapter 4

Call-up

This came rather quicker than I expected. I informed them at my office about my departure and the date I would be leaving. I managed to take a week's holiday at my favourite place, Backbarrow, with my friend Douglas, and I borrowed a small motorbike for 2/6d (12p) for the week.

Petrol rationing had already commenced, so we had to be careful. We had a good time except for the night we motored into Ulverston to go to the cinema. When we came out, Douglas's tyre had been slit with a knife. We removed the wheel, and I set off with it on my handlebars to go to a garage in Greenodd, which I thought would be open late. It was now dark, and I was within 100 yards of the garage when a Special Constable stopped me. The result was that I received a summons to appear in Ulverston Magistrates' Court a week or two after I got home. The man in the garage at Greenodd repaired the tyre, and with the special constable's permission, I drove back to Ulverston. We refitted the wheel, were mobile again, and returned to

Ken (front) with his friend Douglas Maxwell

Backbarrow. The summons was for driving in the dark without a head-light mask. The summons was an earth-shattering experience, and I spoke to Mr Barker (in whose house we were staying). As I did not have the money or opportunity to travel again to Ulverston, he advised me to write to the Clerk of the Court and apologise for my prospective absence from court.

Mr Barker attended court as a spectator and told me that there were three fellows all on the same charge. The first was fined a sum of 5s (25p), the second was fined the sum of one pound, and I, whose case came up third, must have annoyed the Magistrate, who declared that these criminal acts must be stopped immediately and fined me the sum of two pounds! I received a notification at home to pay the fine by a specific date, and wondered how on earth I could raise two pounds. Eventually, I had to approach Mother on the matter and say that I did not have two pounds. Her reply was quite simple. She told me that I would have to go to jail! After a couple of days of wondering what on earth I would do, she relented and gave me a postal order for two pounds, which I despatched immediately. Talk about learning a lesson!

The day of my departure to join the RAF came around, and I arose early to get my things together.

Mother came to the front door with me, and there were the usual parental instructions about what to do and what not to do. As one would expect, the parting was rather bereft of demonstrative emotion, and as I reached the front gate, I turned to wave goodbye. However, I was somewhat troubled by the serious shortage of cash, and I returned to the front steps and said that I had only got fifteen shillings (75p). The reply ran true to form - "Well....MAKE IT DO!" - and, of course, I did.

Ken with mother Edith, and grandmother Albina at the back

Armed with my little attache case containing washing gear and a change of clothing, I presented my railway warrant at Blackpool North. My destination by train was Torquay, and I was to report to the RAF

Reception at a hotel in Babbacombe. The train journey was via Crewe, Bristol, and Torquay and was uneventful. Trains and services were already suffering, and the journey took all day and well into the evening. On the train from Bristol, a vicar and his wife joined me in the compartment, who engaged me in conversation and asked me where I was going. "To join the RAF," I said. "To train to be a Pilot/Air Observer." In other words, if you failed the pilot's course at any time, you were transferred to a navigation course; if you failed, you became a Wireless Operator/Air Gunner. In other words, they had got you and did not intend to let go. During this aircrew training chat, the vicar's wife immediately broke down in tears, and her sobbing continued for a long time. I couldn't quite understand why, but she pressed a note into my hand with their name and address on it and extracted a promise from me that I would go and stay with them at their home as often as possible. It was a lovely, homely thought, but I never saw them again and have forgotten where their home was.

Arriving at Torquay Station late evening, we were rounded up by a keen-eyed Corporal who was obviously on the lookout for youths carrying parcels or attache cases. We were escorted outside the station, where a canvas-topped lorry awaited us. In we went. Arriving at Babbacombe, we were shepherded into a large hotel, and our names were marked off a list of recruits. We were then served a meal and informed of our accommodation for the next two weeks. Mine was the Downs Hotel on the promenade. We were half-walked and half-marched there and allocated a bed. I was in a small front bedroom with two other lads. I was somewhat disgusted with the requisitioned "hotel", which had been stripped of everything - carpets, curtains, furniture, the lot - and had received in exchange spring bed frames, each with three hard, stuffed, square mattresses totalling six feet in length, two sheets, and two blankets, plus a rough pillow. We soon learned that the square mattresses were called "biscuits," no doubt due to the similarity with ships' hardtack biscuits.

Service life had commenced. Little did I know that it would carry on for nearly seven and a half years.

Chapter 5

Induction

We were roused by the noisy Corporal and told that it was time to wash, shave, dress, and be on parade outside the "hotel" in half an hour. Looking around, I noticed that although we were all different shapes and sizes, we did conform to a minimum and maximum dimension. We were all much of a muchness and of various dialects. However, there was a sprinkling of the public school type; I suppose this was the first time I had encountered the breed. Their speech was upmarket but not in the least annoying, and they exuded an air of confidence about the new life, which we did not. I presume that this confidence was born from their experience so far in life in a boarding school or university, away from the sheltered life of home. However, we soon caught up with them in that respect, and it was surprising how quickly one settled down, even during the two weeks of induction.

The Downs "Hotel"

After a short lecture outside the "hotel" by the Corporal, we were formed into a squad of about forty recruits, and the lessons in marching began. Eventually, we arrived at a larger hotel and filed into a spacious dining room, which would serve as our mess hall for the next two weeks. Lining up to receive our "irons" — a knife, fork, dessert spoon, and a metal dixie (a rectangular dish with deep sides and a handle) — we were told this kit was essential for survival and should be guarded carefully. The dixie was meant for any liquid sustenance, such as soup or tea, though soup was rarely on offer. From there, we queued at a long serving table where cooks ladled out porridge and whatever else was available that day. With our food in hand, we made our way to tables and benches to eat. After the meal, plates and irons were washed in large vats of hot water, then rinsed in a separate vat.

Back to our seats, and several boxes of metal stamps and hammers. We had to stamp our irons with our Service Numbers, which we had been issued, and again warned that our numbers must be engraved upon our memories. Mine - I have never forgotten - was 1119287. I might say at this point that our rank was that of AC2. In other words, Aircraftman Second Class. This denoted that we had adopted the status of the lowest form of life in the RAF. More drill and marching followed until lunchtime and again until teatime. So ended the first day.

The next day, we were issued a uniform: a forage cap (which I always found difficult to place safely on my head), a tunic and trousers, two pairs of socks, two shirts, two vests, two pairs of underpants, a pair of boots, and a greatcoat. Instructions were provided on how to wear these items, and any irregular uniform dimensions were promptly altered. We were inspected the next day to establish that our uniforms fit more or less, and we were given brown paper, string, and a label. We wrapped our civilian clothing in these parcels, and they were dispatched to our homes. We were also given a "housewife," pronounced "hussif". With this came a kit bag and instructions on how to label our clothing items— this was something we did in the evenings. Inoculations came shortly afterwards and included an FFI. This was a medical examination of our private parts to ensure that we were Free From Infection. We stood in line in the nude whilst a doctor walked along the line with a short stick. With this instrument, he pushed our genitalia up and down and side to side to look for signs of dirt or disease. This was somewhat disconcerting at the time, but since everyone was treated in the same manner, it was not a significant problem.

Now fully-fledged and uniformed members, the two weeks or what remained of it were spent becoming proficient in drill, marching, and saluting practice. One morning, we were informed that we were to attend a lecture on VD after breakfast. "What's VD?" we asked the Corporal, who replied, "You'll find out soon." Our ignorance pointed to our innocence about such things as sex and venereal disease.

Our evenings were occupied mainly by polishing our buttons and boots until they shone like glass. As far as I know, nobody ever went into the town of Babbacombe. However, I suppose that the wealthy types would slope off to a pub or cafe or such. However, most of us were impoverished, and the capital we had slowly disappeared as we bought shoe polish, toothpaste, and other essentials. My 15s (75p) soon went that way. Our pay was 2s (10p) per day, but we were paid every two weeks, so our first pay parade was at the end of our stay at Babbacombe.

I have mentioned before that I did not take kindly to the primitive lifestyle at the Downs "Hotel", so I developed a plan, and looking back on it, I wonder and marvel at the astounding cheek of it. I went on a short expedition along Downs Road, where our hotel was located. All the hotels had been requisitioned except one at the road's end. This was the Cliffs Hotel, now known as the Churchill Hotel. I entered and went to the reception desk. "The RAF has sent me to see if you have any accommodation," I said. "They have run out of beds."

Ken's preferred accomodation, the Cliffs Hotel (Now Churchill Hotel)

To my surprise and delight, they said yes, so I went to get my things. In hindsight, the proprietors were well aware of my intentions, but they never said a word. Instead, they showed me to a bedroom containing two single beds. What luxury! A Sergeant Pilot occupied the other bed. He was on a week's rest, although I didn't talk to him much, as he spent most of the time asleep. I told the hotel that all I required was a bed, and that the RAF would provide me with food. I stayed in this luxury for five or six days, getting up early to be on parade in front of the Downs "Hotel". I recall being invited to have breakfast or dinner on occasion. I accepted this with many thanks. Perhaps they felt very sorry for me, but for my part, I was enjoying the change in my circumstances. Remarkably, no one split on me, and at the end of the week, I told the proprietor that he must send the bill to the RAF. I wonder if he ever did - or whether he wrote it off as doing a good turn. I thanked him sincerely and departed to join the rest.

The fortnight ended, and we had been "inducted". We were told that we would be departing by train to join No. 7 ITW at Newquay, Cornwall. ITW means "Initial Training Wing". I recall having a brief conversation with my roommate at the luxurious Cliffs Hotel - the Sergeant Pilot who was on rest. One night, I went to my room and asked him what it was like being a pilot. His reply was curt but to the point. "The best thing you can do," he said, "is keep out of it!" Although this advice turned out later to be very good and accurate, it was unheeded. He went back to sleep, undoubtedly to regain his strength and composure after his onerous duties in the Battle of Britain, which had recently ended.

Chapter 6

Aircrew Ground School

We arrived at Newquay and were marched to our new place of residence—the Beachview Hotel on the cliffs. Back to earth again with the same bare building, I was allocated one of the smaller bedrooms, which contained three beds. These were purely sleeping quarters—there being, as in Babbacombe, a central dining room, but this time, in addition, a school room.

The course here lasted eight weeks, and the lessons, or Ground School, took up four or five hours per day, with the usual drill, or "square bashing" as it was called, filling in the rest of our time. We were now introduced to a routine I abhorred- guard duty outside the hotel.

I cannot recall how many times this cycle occurred, but the night duty consisted of two hours on guard and two hours of sleep. I loathed it, and during the night, we were visited while on guard to ensure we were doing our job. It was now October or November, and the nights were cold and miserable. I wondered if it were possible to sleep whilst standing up with a rifle on the hotel's steps, but I was afraid to try. Dereliction of duty was a severely punishable offence, and I do not remember anyone being caught. Later in my training, I was threatened with a charge of Mutiny - but more of that when the narrative reaches that point.

There were eight subjects taught in Ground School: Air Force Law,

Meteorology, Signals (Morse code), Engines, the Theory of Flight, Air Navigation, Armaments, and Aircraft Recognition.

Air Force Law covered basic topics concerning discipline, including who to salute and when, the comparative ranks of the Air Force, the Army, and the Navy, as well as Court Martial, Courts of Enquiry, and other related matters.

Meteorology was very interesting, covering cloud formations and names, winds, line squalls, fronts, isobars, and more. It also included learning how to recognise weather systems in the making and which clouds to avoid when flying.

Signals involved learning Morse code, which involved sending and receiving messages using a buzzer and Aldis lamp. To pass the examination, you had to send and receive a minimum of eight words per minute.

Armament was learning the various types of guns, with emphasis on the Browning Machine Gun. It was learning how to recognise why the gun had stopped firing, whether it was one, two, or three stoppages, and what to do about it. The gun had to be completely stripped down and reassembled within a specific time frame.

Aircraft Recognition is self-explanatory and was tested in daylight and low-light conditions using drawings and photographs.

Air Navigation was learned using the Dead Reckoning system, which involves the triangle of velocities and trigonometry. It involved calculating the direction and speed of the wind while ostensibly in flight, adjusting the aircraft's course to reach the destination, and calculating the ETA, or Estimated Time of Arrival.

Engines were the mechanical components of internal combustion engines, including both two-stroke and four-stroke engines, as well as ignition, cooling, and other related systems.

The Theory of Flight, as its name implies, is about understanding why aircraft can fly at all, given that they are heavier than air. As far as I know, it remains a theory, although it appears to work very well.

Again, most of our spare time was spent tending to our uniforms, with occasional visits to a small cafe to spend our hard-earned 10p per day on cups of tea and buns, and playing the record player incessantly with records such as "The Woodchoppers' Ball" by Woody Herman.

So, life at the ITW progressed until I had an upset. I was playing rugby against a team from No. 5 ITW, based in Newquay, when I was picked up and swung around by a chap of immense stature. I fell to the ground, and he fell on top of me. I heard the crack and soon discovered that my leg had broken. I retired to the sidelines. After the match, I had no option but to walk back to the hotel, complaining bitterly. I was allowed to walk back at my own pace, which was a "generous" concession. The next morning, after a sleepless night, I reported sick. I was the only one and was told to report to the Sick Quarters, some distance away, at another requisitioned hotel. I remember the name "The Bolothas" - a peculiar name for a hotel that housed a peculiar doctor. He was young and obviously recently qualified. He examined my leg, pronounced that I had pulled a muscle, and gave me a chit for Light Duties. I walked back. I knew he was wrong. I remained as motionless as possible, and the next day, I walked again to the Sick Quarters. Again, I was examined by the same doctor who reaffirmed his diagnosis.

I walked back, and as soon as I saw the Corporal, I vented my feelings about my leg. Luckily, he believed me and ordered an ambulance. Thank God! I was taken to the other end of town, along the south side of the bay, to a huge hotel that had been converted into a hospital. There, I was X-rayed, and they found that my ankle was indeed fractured. I had my leg put into a plaster from below the knee to my toes and put to bed. However, after a couple of days, I was told to get up and see if I could walk about on a plastered leg, which incorporated a metal hoop to use as a heel. I managed it OK and was given a week's leave and a railway warrant for a return trip to Blackpool. I bid farewell to the other course members and caught my train. At Newton Abbot, I had to change trains and catch the Penzance to Crewe train. There was not one vacant seat in sight, although I walked through the crowded corridors to try and find somewhere to sit, and ended up sitting on the floor at the end of a corridor. Incredibly, the journey to Blackpool took twenty-three and a half hours. Was I glad to get home and rest!

The week soon went by, and I returned to the hospital, where the plaster was eventually removed after six weeks. In the meantime, I rejoined No.8 ITW and continued the Ground School, more or less where I had left off. Some great news was that being in plaster for 6 weeks relieved me of marching, drill, and guard duty. There was at least some benefit. The return to the hospital to have the plaster removed was quickly done, and I then had to recondition the unused muscles. I walked whenever possible to get my muscles back in shape. At the end of the course, the written exams came, and I was successful.

Before we left Newquay, those who had passed (most of the course, I think) were promoted—fantastic. We had to sew our new rank badges on the sleeves of our tunics and greatcoats. We were now LACs (Leading Aircraftsmen), and our pay shot up to 6s (30p) per day. I was posted (along with about 30 others) to an EFTS whose number I have since forgotten. This stood for Elementary Flying Training School and was located at Staverton, on the main road between Gloucester and Cheltenham.

Ground School, Newquay. Ken frot row, far right

Chapter 7

Elementary Flying Training School

As it turned out, Staverton was not really an RAF Station. The RAF contingent was a tiny offshoot in one corner of the airfield, comprised of three barrack-type buildings: a dormitory, an ablution block, and a dispersal hut.

I cannot recall what dining accommodation was provided. The entire area consisted of the factory building of the Gloucester Aircraft Company and a grassy airfield. The Gloucester Aircraft Company was famous for the pre-war (very pre-war) Gloucester Gladiator. This was a biplane armed with machine guns - a single-seater. There were three of these that became famous during the siege of Malta: "Faith," "Hope," and "Charity." They did sterling work before Malta received Hurricanes and, much later on, Spitfires.

Our unit had two or three old training planes called Tiger Moths, and the flying instructors were actually civilians—not military men. My instructor was a friendly fellow in his mid-forties, which felt ancient to me at the time. The Tiger Moth was a simple, open-cockpit biplane with two seats—one in front for the student and one behind for the instructor. The engine sat just in front of us, and the fuel tank was mounted above our heads on the top wing, feeding fuel to the engine by gravity. Everything about the aircraft was basic. There were no brakes, and it cruised along at about 60 miles per hour. The speed was displayed on a small metal flap that bent backwards as we flew, indicating a scale to show our speed. Inside the cockpit, there were just a few instruments: a compass, a simple gauge for climbing or turning, and dials for oil pressure and engine temperature. You controlled the plane using a throttle, a joystick that felt surprisingly flimsy, and a foot bar to steer the rudder. To start the engine, you didn't press a button—we had to get out and swing the propeller by hand, which was part of our training. There was no radio either. To get your instructor's attention, you blew down a speaking tube that ran between the two cockpits. The blast of air made a whistle, letting him know you wanted to say something.

We were equipped with flying boots, gauntlets, a flying suit, and a helmet that incorporated earpieces attached to the speaking tube. The cockpits were open to the wind, each with a small windshield. We strapped on our parachutes, and we also strapped ourselves into the aircraft. These were checked before takeoff by a member of the ground crew who was also responsible for removing the chocks from in front of the wheels upon instruction from the pilot once the engine had started.

Ground School lectures in the dispersal hut included a new subject: Airmanship.

This included starting, taxiing, and takeoff procedures. One always had to take off and land into the wind, as indicated by several windsocks around the airfield. Other lessons included Emergency Landing procedures and passing other aircraft in the air. As in sea navigation, the rule was to keep the port side (left) to the port side. During flying, we were constantly looking for suitable places to land, and several times during the initial flying instruction, the instructor would suddenly cut the throttle and shout down the tube, "Engine failure, land it!"

We had to choose a suitable field or space to put it down. The wind direction was judged by washing on lines, smoke from chimneys, etc. A series of "S" bends were performed to correct the approach and skim over the hedge to land. The instructor would open the throttle a few feet from the ground and praise or curse you according to your efforts. If I remember correctly, we flew around at about 2000 ft—perhaps a little less than that.

Each pupil was allowed eight hours of dual instruction, and if you had not reached a sufficiently capable standard by then, it was "curtains", and off you went to join a course for navigators, air gunners, or wireless operators—an utter disappointment for those who failed.

If you had been successful after eight hours, then the instructor told you to land 15 minutes into your next flight. He'd get out, pat you on the shoulder, and say: "It's all yours, do a takeoff and landing". He stood on the ground and watched, and on your return, he would hopefully tell you to do three more circuits and bumps. Having completed these, you would return for the verdict. Success brought a tremendous sigh of relief, and a further two or three hours flying solo were undertaken.

We did not fly from Staverton Airfield, but each day, we travelled by coach to Worcester Airfield and spent the entire day there. Then, we returned by coach at the end of the day's proceedings. Worcester was a quiet airfield, which suited the purpose better than Staverton, as it was busy with larger aircraft.

One day, a notable event occurred in Worcester. We arrived by coach to find an aircraft parked there - and what was it? No less than a Spitfire Mark I. I rushed over to inspect it and marvelled at it. I climbed onto the wing to look into the cockpit. What a complex array of knobs, switches, levers and instruments. That settles it - I thought, I will never fly something like this! It's far too complicated. After the shock of seeing inside the cockpit, I thought, well, other fellows could do it - why not me? But such private confidence hid my true feelings of doubt. After all, we were not yet pilots - far from it- we had simply learned a little about what it feels like to be airborne and to fly around, and then return safely, if sometimes rather awkwardly, to terra firma.

However, so far, so good. We were introduced to an instrument called, believe it or not, a "computer", or more specifically, an airspeed and course computer. We learned to estimate the time of arrival by plotting data on a map. The computer was strapped to the upper leg and had various dials and controls. It was meant to be innovative, but I never saw one again after training.

And so we enjoyed our solo flights after the scrutinised circuits and bumps around the airfield. Short cross-country jaunts were delightful, and we continually practised looking out for a suitable place to force land should the occasion arise, which, thank goodness, it never did, at least not until much later in my flying career. By the end of this course, I had amassed the princely total of, if I recall, sixteen flying hours. Wonderful!

Our postings came through on cue, and mine was to a Service Flying Training School (SFTS) at Montrose on the east coast of Scotland, north of Perth. We went by train - I cannot remember how many were in the party.

Chapter 8

Service Flying Training School

In 1941, Montrose was a pleasant small town, and we occasionally visited there during our time off, which was nice, especially since we didn't get very much of it.

Ground School continued, and as you will appreciate, the subjects became more comprehensive. We were still regimented and disciplined with the usual drill, boot and button polishing, and weekly kit inspections. These latter ones were a nuisance but still formed an integral part of the training.

Our rank was still LAC, although we were now receiving an extra 1/6d (7p) per day flying pay. This extra enabled us to buy eggs, bacon, and chips on our occasional trips to Montrose. The memory of these delightful meals has never left me. I do not know how the little cafe managed to secure its supplies of these foods during the severe rationing, nor did I care.

During this course, I managed to save the princely sum of £7 to buy myself an object I had not owned before - a wristwatch. This may seem a rather simple pleasure these days, given that children often own a wristwatch by the time they are five years old.

It was my pride and joy. It was called Roamer and was gold-plated. A couple of weeks later, I had saved sufficient money to have my name and home address engraved on the inside back cover. Wonderful. The pleasure abruptly ended when, some short time later, somehow, somewhere, somebody relieved me of my possession. I reported it with a complete description to my superiors, but it was never seen again, at least not by me. Utter sadness - but my only benefit was a lesson in being far more careful.

Together with most of my pupils, I thought our training had some peculiar aspects. These were the odd guard duty, fire picket, spud-bashing, and other duties of an unpleasant nature in the kitchens. I suppose they all came under the heading of discipline. Punishment for offending against the rules was usually given in the form of one of the above, as well as loss of pay and being confined to camp.

Displayed daily on the notice board in the barrack hut were the Daily Routine Orders (DROs). These informed you of any changes to the routine. At the end were lists of names for guard duty, fire picket, spud-bashing*, and other assignments. If one was confined to camp or had had some other punishment, then one's name and punishment were displayed for all to see. This, of course, caused a deal of merriment amongst those who, at the time, were blameless, which brings me to a subheading for the chapter:

MUTINY

This word, in itself, is, I suppose, harmless enough, but when you carefully consider its meaning and consequences, it becomes terrifying. Lately, I have read the true story of "Mutiny on the Bounty" via my talking book machine - a fascinating book that also brought this tale back to mind.

Part of our daily routine was to be awakened by the "distinguished" Corporal at the unearthly hour of 6:30 am to be marshalled outside in the cold, early light of day and forced to perform the motions of Physical Training (PT). To me, it was a dreadful, entirely unnecessary routine. I hated it, as did most of us.

Somewhere deep within me is a determination to disobey rules,

---

* *Guard duty, fire picket, and spud-bashing* were common military tasks: security shifts patrolling the base, fire watch to prevent or respond to fires, and potato peeling as a routine chore or punishment.

which occasionally surfaces. Overall, this determination to disobey the rules and heed common sense has saved my life, but on this occasion, it did not save my life; it paved the way for a most frightening interview. Bear in mind that we were on active service during a state of emergency, as they called the war. Nevertheless, my friend and I, who occupied the next bed to mine, decided to opt out of the PT call and have an extra hour in bed - what a luxury! But all good things come to an end, and upon the Squad's return, we were immediately confronted by the Corporal. I may say here that the rank of Corporal was the next above us, but the distance between was immeasurable.

His instruction was brief and to the point. "You two report to the orderly room immediately after breakfast". The pleasure of the extra hour in bed had suddenly disappeared, and we duly reported as ordered. The Administration Officer in charge of the course informed us that we were to be interviewed by the Station Commander, a Group Captain, and we were immediately escorted to his office.

We wished we had been good boys, but it was too late. We marched into his office, stood to attention, and saluted. The officer explained to this high-ranking disciplinarian what we had done. We stood there in fear and trembling. He regarded us with a stony stare and started his severe reprimand. This in itself was bad enough, but when he told us that it was within his power to charge us with mutiny, we shrank with horror. He explained to us that on active service during a war, the punishment was death by shooting. He then left the room with the Administration Officer, leaving us standing there, sweating. After what seemed a lifetime, they returned, and the Group Captain sat and faced us.

"There is no doubt you are both guilty," he said. "I do not need a court-martial to tell me that. You both agree, don't you?" "Yes, Sir," we said in unison and waited again for the outcome. He lectured us yet again and then told us that he would be lenient, as this was the first time we had caused any trouble. We were confined to camp for three weeks and had numerous guard duties, fire pickets, kitchen chores, and the constant reminder of "God help us if we disobey again." We were marched out and went through another tirade from the Corporal, who vowed to watch us at all times. We believed him. We applied ourselves diligently to our punishments, relieved to find we were still alive. It had taught us a valuable lesson.

Like the previous course at Staverton, we did not actually fly from Montrose but from a satellite airfield at Edzell, some twenty miles northwest.

37 Course, Montrose. Ken sits at bottom right.

The aircraft here was a Miles Master I, immeasurably more powerful, with two enclosed cockpits. It felt, as indeed it was, a much bigger machine and of all-metal construction compared with the wood and fabric of the Tiger Moth. Moreover, it also had a retractable undercarriage. The central blind flying instrument panel was surrounded by more sophisticated instruments relevant to a more powerful engine.

The trainee again occupied the front cockpit. All the data concerning takeoff, landing, and stall speeds were learned and tested. We learned about everyday flying, together with the more advanced aerobatics. One day, before takeoff, the instructor explained how to completely pull over an internal canvas cover to exclude any daylight and maintain complete darkness. Once the requisite height had been attained, I drew over the cover to learn the method of blind flying. "Just fly straight and level, and keep your speed constant," the instructor said. "That's all." The art of blind flying, flying purely by watching the instruments, is not particularly easy to master. Weird sensations make one think that the aircraft is diving, climbing, or turning, especially in strong winds. "Watch the instruments," he kept saying. It was unpleasant, but eventually, I succeeded and gained an essential qualification. One which, given the changeable weather in that part of the world, was indeed an art that had to be learned as soon as possible, and I had to use it many times during my flying career.

This blind flying was also practised on the ground using a "Link Trainer," which is still used today, although I suppose more advanced models are now available. Navigation exercises around specified points on the map were also tested. I think we had progressed to internal and external radio communication on this aircraft. Things were getting a bit tougher, but they were also very interesting. We underwent another rigorous medical test during the course, including a lung performance test. This involved an instrument somewhat like the present blood pressure tester. A rubber tube connected one end of the "U" tube of mercury to a glass mouthpiece. A clip was placed on the nostrils, and the test involved blowing the mercury to a specified point on the scale and then holding it there for an extended period. Something in the order of 30 to 45 seconds, I believe. Dreadful, but it had to be done.

Ground School and the usual drill and PT were continued. Solo flying became standard until the big day arrived: We had our Wings Flying Test. The ground subjects exams had been completed, so it was just the flying. By the end of the week, we would know whether or not we were qualified pilots. The poor souls who failed were given a second chance. A further unsuccessful result meant that they were then on the Navigation and other aircrew courses. Together with the flying test results, we would receive a notification about our promotions. This was a farcical and straightforward procedure, and I should think, particularly British. If you were educated in grammar school, then you were promoted to Sergeant. If you were from a public school or University, you were commissioned and promoted to Pilot Officer (PO). Nothing whatsoever to do with flying ability. At this point, the branch of flying you were destined for was also decided. Fighter Command, Bomber Command, Coastal Command, etc. I assume they assessed your personality and flying to obtain the answer.

The big day came, and we crowded around the notice board. I was there! Sergeant Ken Cam, posted to an Operational Training Unit (OTU) at RAF Hawarden, near Chester, to fly Spitfires. Great delight! That night, we (the Sergeants) removed the propellers on our arms denoting LAC (Leading Aircraftsman) and sewed on our Sergeant's stripes. Those who passed and were posted to Fighter Command were allowed a few hours on a Mark I Hurricane. This was front-line stuff and very exciting! Flying it was easier than I had imagined, and of course, there was only one seat, so there was no dual instruction. It was a tremendous feeling to get it off the ground, fly it around, and land it. We were very elated.

During one of these flights in the Hurricane, I was aerobatting over Perth, and somehow, for the only time I was flying, I ended up in a flat spin. Now, an ordinary downward spin is easy enough to recover from. Close the throttle, ease the stick fully forward, and apply hard rudder to the left or right opposite to the direction of the spin. However, there is no procedure to recover from a flat spin, where the aircraft spins but remains horizontal. There is no answer, but of course, in a mounting panic, I tried everything—all to no avail. Baling out of the plane in a horizontal position was fraught with danger, but it was the only option that offered a slim chance of survival. The gods were with me that day, and luckily, I hit a sudden vertical air current that sufficiently tilted a wing to put me back in control. I immediately took the thing back and landed. I shall never forget the airspace over Perth.

Back on land, I bade farewell to the Corporal (whom I had now out-ranked), and he generously wished me the best of luck.

Chapter 9

Operational Training Unit

I had made a good friendship with a Scotsman who hailed from Dumfries. Despite being given only four days' leave—how generous!—he spent two days at his home and then joined me in Warbreck Drive, Blackpool, for the remaining two days. So we travelled to Hawarden together.

Our promotion to Sergeant Pilot gave us a tremendous rise in pay. We now received 12/6d (62p) per day, including the statutory 1/6 (7p) per day flying pay. We were wealthy!

In six weeks, we thought we would be operational fighter pilots. Little did we know that the operations in France, including Dunkirk, and the Battle of Britain in late summer 1940, together with the continued air offensive, had sadly depleted the Fighter Pilot Force. Consequently, our six-week course at the Operational Training Unit was cut to three weeks. This appeared to be a stupid move, but I suppose the hierarchy knew what it was doing. However, as we later discovered, it was very costly due to the use of half-trained pilots.

The Spitfires here were well-worn Mark Is with the occasional Mark II. A dummy cockpit provided a cockpit drill and radio, and we learned code words, such as "quilt," "mattress," and "Popeye," denoting our relationship with cloud formations. We did all the stuff on the ground, and then came the big day when we were let loose in the famous Spitfire. On the Mark I model, there was a lever to select up or down for the undercarriage, and a long lever that, after choosing up or down, had to be pumped back and forth to supply hydraulic power.

Spotting a pilot on his first solo was easy and caused merriment amongst the onlookers. Once the wheels were off the ground, the aircraft proceeded as though on a fast big dipper until the wheels were locked in the "up" position. Practice, of course, overcame this and resulted in a smooth climb.

This was now flying in the true sense of the word, a fast, up-to-date machine that was very responsive to the controls. The Spitfire was, at first, not an easy machine to land and take off. Immediately after full power was given to take off, the aircraft would swing hard to the right, necessitating a hard left rudder to keep it straight. As the speed for takeoff was reached and the thing became airborne, the rudder was gradually removed, and straight flight was achieved. On landing, with the undercarriage being so narrow, one had to ensure that the approach to the grass or runway was strictly level. Also, because of the long engine in front of you, you lost forward vision when you brought the nose up for the landing position, so you had to judge the height above the ground via the side of the aircraft. Tricky, to say the least.

Hawarden was peculiar in that it was subject to sudden bouts of mist or fog, and one Sunday afternoon, we lost seven of the pilots who came to grief either in the hills or on landing. What a blow—It was disastrous! Especially given the significant shortage of fully trained men. I was caught one day in these adverse conditions, and luckily, I decided to fly westward over the sea until I was clear of the fog. I descended to a low but safe altitude and flew obliquely towards the coast, turning north and following the coastline until I reached the canal and river. I flew along this course until I spotted the aerodrome and landed safely. Those gods again had been with me.

We had a brief session with the instructor from the previous course on low flying, and although it wasn't very low, it was still exciting! However, low flying at the OTU was strictly - I repeat - *strictly* forbidden! This order, I suppose, made it all the more attractive! One day, the attraction overcame common sense, and I gave it a try. Turning in from the sea, I came down very low over the Promenade at West Kirby on the Wirral peninsula and down onto the sand. I was *really* low, as will be evident from the story. I was wearing a pair of regulation-issue silk gloves, which were intended to be worn under gauntlet gloves, but I never did.

During this low-flying session, a finger of the silk glove became lodged in the throttle groove, and I shoved the throttle backwards and forwards to dislodge it. A sudden forward motion of the throttle resulted in the nose of the aircraft going downwards, and to my horror, I hit the sand. There was an awful crunching sound, and I had cut about six or eight inches off the propeller blades! The handling became extraordinarily rough, and I cursed my stupidity. I staggered back to the aerodrome, thinking hard as to what my excuse could be. By the time I had got the thing on the ground, I had made up my mind. Say nothing and pretend I knew nothing about it. I got out, and before I had gone many yards, there was a shout from the fitter - I ignored it. I sat in the dispersal hut in fear and trepidation, and soon, the Flight Commander came to me and said, "Report to the Station Commander tomorrow at 9:00 a.m. with your flying logbook." He did not have to say any more. I knew I was grounded and had finished my career as a pilot. What a disaster!

I returned to my billet to make up my mind as to what I was going to do. There was no doubt about the outcome of an interview with the Group Captain, and I was very despondent. This was halfway through the third week of a six-week course, and we had been informed the previous day that the course would conclude at the end of the week. The previous day, we had been given our railway warrants and our postings. My Scottish friend and I were destined for No. 234 Fighter Squadron at RAF Ibsley in Hampshire. So I sat there and made my decision. Here was that streak of rebellion again. "I'm off," I told myself.

I packed my kit and left. I got a lift to the station and went home for the rest of the week! Believe it or not, I never heard another word, although I expected a recall at any time. But it never came. I do not know whether or not the Group Captain thought I'd be a "dead duck" anyway, as the life expectancy of a fighter pilot at that time was a few weeks, sometimes even a few days, but made I it on the due date and arrived at RAF Ibsley to join the No. 234 Spitfire Squadron.

Chapter 10

The First Fighter Squadron

The wartime railway journeys were lengthy and uncomfortable, and we arrived at RAF Ibsley in the early hours of the morning. We were picked up by a lorry at the nearest railway station. There were four of us, my Scottish friend and two other fellows from the OTU. I asked them whether they had heard anything about my untimely and sudden departure, but there was no news. I prayed that the whole episode would fade out, and seemingly it did. There were now far more pressing and urgent matters to consider.

We were allocated a room each in one of the half-dozen barrack huts, some of which were half a mile from the aerodrome and hidden among the trees. You will notice a significant change in our lifestyles here. We were now Sergeants, and like the Officers, we had a room to ourselves. The furniture was standard - a bed, a table, a chair, a wardrobe, and a coke-burning stove that used to belch fumes interminably.

It was the winter of 1941/42. I forget which side of the New Year it was, but it was chilly, and every evening after the meal (now, of course, in the Sergeants' Mess), we would gather bits of wood and light our stoves. I was very fortunate in my allocation of a room, as it contained a wind-up gramophone and about a dozen 78 RPM records. The records were all of bands like Glenn Miller, Tommy Dorsey, Woody Herman, and bands of that era, and I must say that in the rigorous days to come, they really kept me going. The equipment had belonged to a pilot who, the week before, had come to grief and no longer required it. Sad indeed - very sad, but an occurrence that one quickly grew accustomed to over the coming days and weeks. I was still a non-drinker; in hindsight, this was extremely stupid. To have let one's hair down every evening, I feel, would have been much more of a benefit than abstinence. However, that is how it was.

There were three Spitfire squadrons on the aerodrome—234, 111, and I think 601—so these comprised a Wing. The Wing Commander was a small chap (ex-Battle of Britain) whose name I remember but will not quote. He finished his flying career and his life in Tunisia, and, according to a book I read, is buried outside Tunis.

No 234 Squadron, April 1942. Ken is second from the left

We (the new entrants) were told to report to the Squadron Leader's office at 9:00 am—another Battle of Britain man, who was very pleasant. I was the first one to be interviewed. After asking which OTU I had attended, he inquired about the number of flying hours I had accumulated. "Forty-six," I said, and his mouth dropped open. "Good God," was his reply. "How many on Spitfires?" I told him it was around 15, and that the OTU course had been reduced from six to three weeks. "How's your air-firing?" he asked. "I don't see any comments here on your papers." "I haven't even fired a gun yet," I answered.

I do not know who was the more crestfallen - he or I. "Well," he said, "You've a lot to learn about flying a Spitfire this morning—this afternoon, you'll be on operations. I can allow you an hour's flying before lunch". I saluted and turned away, leaving his office feeling rather despondent. I was a fighter pilot now, or was about to be after lunch! The ability to fly an aeroplane well suddenly became an essential ability. But what was the difference between the flying I had already done and the flying I was about to do? In short, a world of difference.

Flying a fighter aeroplane as an aeroplane, and flying a fighter aeroplane as *a fighter* bear little resemblance to each other. I was shown where the 234 Squadron Disposal huts were and told I was to be in "A" Flight. I went down to meet the Flight Commander, whom I did not get to know very well, as he came to grief over Cherbourg a few days later. He took me out, showed me a Spitfire, and said: "That's yours." I looked at the markings "AZ-A". "AZ" were the squadron letters, and "A" was the letter denoting that plane. I was pleased, and the thought went through my head that these letters surely meant "The beginning and the end." Perhaps I would be lucky after all.

Ken's aeroplane

As far as I could tell, it was a new plane and a Mark VB. The differences between the Mark Vs and the Mark I and II were impressive even to my very limited knowledge. It had four Browning .303 machine guns and two cannons. It had a variable-pitch propeller, either a Rotol laminated wood propeller or a de Havilland metal one. The radio was a four-channel push-button type, and it also featured a significantly improved system for raising and lowering the undercarriage, eliminating the need for a long pump handle to be pushed backwards and forward. A simple movement of a short lever was all that was necessary. The Mark VA had eight machine guns, and the Mark VC had four cannons. The Mark V had a three-position gun button, allowing one to select machine guns, cannons, or the lot at once!

The Flight Commander left me to it, and I studied the array of clocks, levers, and switches. A "SAFE" button for the guns and a brake lever were also on the control column. Having somewhat satisfied myself with the arrangement of controls, I went back to the dispersal hut.

Inside the cockpit of a Spitfire Mark V

Introductions to the other flight members were made, and I was given a parachute and a Mae West (an inflatable life jacket worn by pilots and aircrew). Inscribed on the Mae West were the words "Young Jed." I never found out who "Young Jed" was, although I kept the Mae West as my property. I also got a new flying helmet, which, of course, housed earphones, tinted goggles, a cable and jack plug for the radio, and a flexible tube to connect to the oxygen supply.

I was approached by another Sergeant, Rover McLeod, who hailed from Calgary, Canada. I was to share my hours of instruction with him. "We'll take off together," he said, "and we'll get up to about six thousand feet. Then get behind and below me as close as you like."

Once we were up there, he motioned for me to get behind him, and then came on the radio. "All you have to do this morning," he said, "is to learn how to keep in that position. Do your best to follow me. Go!" he said, and pulled up sharply and to the left. I did the same, but within a very few seconds, I had absolutely no idea where he was. Amazed, I looked around all over the place, but no sign of him. "Here I am," he said over the radio, "right behind you — you're a dead duck. Now, let's try again. We haven't a great deal of time."

I sweated and kept trying to keep up with him, but in that hour, I had begun to learn how to throw the thing about. I had very mixed feelings about my performance, but on landing, he came over and said, "Not bad. Do your best this afternoon—you'll fly as my number two—look after my tail."

Fortunately, the weather was good, and after lunch, we had a briefing by the Commanding Officer (CO). We were to fly over Cherbourg and around the Normandy coast at twenty-two thousand feet to start with, and "see what we can stir up!" I thought this was asking for trouble, but I was just a new boy.

At this stage in the narrative, it might be advisable to say a little about the method of squadron flying at that stage in the war. The V or Vic formation of three aircraft, with the two planes being one on either side and slightly behind the centre man, was repeated four times; thus, there were four Vics of three aircraft, making the twelve aircraft of the squadron. The front Vic was the CO in the centre, and the two Flight Commanders on either side. The number twos were behind the number ones, and the whole formation was tightly packed. This was the ridiculous part - I soon found out that it was difficult enough to keep tightly in position, let alone look around. Being new, I was the tail man in the right-hand four.

This reminds me that as I left home to join the squadron, my mother gave me two bits of advice: "Keep away from women wearing grass skirts and always fly at the back." I think both bits of advice were inappropriate, especially the second one. In a fighter squadron, one started off at the back, which, of course, was the most dangerous position, and if one lived long enough, one gradually crept to a forward position. Not the best advice, but there we are.

The takeoff was in twos, and as soon as we were airborne, I took my position behind and slightly below my number one, Rover McLeod. The squadron climbed and headed more or less due south up to the specified height. As we knew we were operating at a high level, which was usually the case, we used oxygen immediately after takeoff.

Visibility was excellent as we crossed the Channel. Strict radio silence was always the rule until the enemy was spotted. Fortunately, nothing happened on this, my first operation, and after cruising around for a while, we turned homeward. Was I glad!

Trips in a Spitfire usually lasted between an hour and a quarter and an hour and a half. These times could be lengthened under circumstances such as a convoy patrol where speed and manoeuvring were not essential. Still, conversely, if one was involved in some melee, then the use of fuel power and full boost quickly used up vital petrol supplies. We carried 47 gallons in a tank between the cockpit and the engine. On later Marks, this was increased by fitting tanks in the wings and tail; however, they were slightly larger machines and more powerful, utilising the Griffon engine as opposed to the Merlin engine used in the Mark Vs. Both, of course, were Rolls-Royce power units.

I was very glad indeed to be back safe and sound, and I had been extremely fortunate to have had a peaceful initiation into the life of a fighter pilot. Having deposited my helmet and Mae West in the dispersal hut, I went out to my aircraft to chat with my Fitter, one Freddie Hall from Birmingham. He was a conscientious chap who was with me all the time on 234 Squadron, and he always wanted to know how the plane had performed and what I had encountered.

I told him that the machine behaved perfectly and that I was confident his work would resolve any issues I might encounter. The "trouble" came the very next day, but was indeed through no fault of his own.

The duties of the squadron were as follows:

Fitter Freddie Hall and Ken

- To maintain a section of two aircraft on readiness at all times between dawn and dusk.
- To support offensive operations over and across the English Channel as far as possible in the form of a Flight (six aircraft), a section of two aircraft, a squadron of 12 aircraft or a Wing of three squadrons or a multi-Wing offensive of more than one Wing.
- To escort shipping passing through the Channel or around our shores (a Convoy Patrol).
- To perform low-level attacks (a Rhubarb) on military targets in France, such as aerodromes, railways, fortifications and gun emplacements.

We occasionally escorted larger aircraft on daylight bombing raids, i.e., as far as our limited range would allow, and we were not always informed of the reasons behind our missions. Once, we escorted a plane down the West Coast of France as far as we could. We later found out that Winston Churchill was on that plane, en route to attend a Conference of Leaders in a neutral country.

Practice flying, occasional gunnery exercises, and training with the Army were also conducted. These latter were pleasant enough when no one was shooting at you, yet they formed an essential part of training for all. Dawn readiness involved sleeping in the dispersal hut, and ideally, we were awakened by the on-duty airman in time to be dressed and ready before dawn.

The responsibilities of the airman were to remain by the telephone and sometimes make tea. On a call from the Operations Room, he would immediately sound a Klaxon and telephone the aerodrome control tower. Someone there would shoot a red flare warning into the air, informing everyone that a Section was about to take off and must be given absolute priority for takeoff, which, I must say, was not always down the runway and into the wind. The Ground Crew of the Readiness Section was immediately attentive to the pilots who ran to the aircraft and jumped into the cockpits. The pilot was assisted in strapping on his parachute, which remained in the aircraft, and then securing the aircraft's straps. A "trolley jack" was already plugged in, which avoided using one's aircraft battery to start the engine. The airman would whip out the plug and pull the chocks away as soon as the engine fired. Remembering to close and lock the small side door on a Spitfire was crucial, as once airborne, it became impossible to close the hood. The sliding hood remained open during takeoff and landing, and the seat was raised fully. Once airborne, the hood was closed, and the seat lowered fully. The Section Leader then called the Operations Room: "Red One airborne" or whatever Section colour you were. Back would come the instruction "Vector 180 - Angels 22" or whatever. "Angels" was, of course, the height in thousands of feet. This information would then perhaps be extended with an estimate of the number of enemy aircraft approaching. Radar was extremely helpful, of course, but it was still in its infancy, and its operators were still learning the ropes. However, I don't know where we would have been without this phenomenal invention, which was once again British. But I digress.

After a cup of tea, Rover McLeod came to me and suggested that I might like to have an hour's practice in formation flying. I readily agreed, and after getting permission from the Flight Commander, we took off as a pair. "Keep as close as you can," he said, "I will do some gentle manoeuvre at first, and then we shall open up and try some formation aerobatics. We want to reach the stage when we can fly the two aircraft and manoeuvre as one". I learned a lot in that hour, and we returned to base. "Much better," he said, and I was pleased.

We were not called upon for the rest of the daylight hours, and after a meal, I went back to my room, played some records, thought about the day's experience, and wondered about tomorrow.

Chapter 11

Operations

The truck came to our huts in the woods to take us the half-mile to the mess for breakfast, and then we went to our dispersal at the far end of the aerodrome. The dawn readiness Section had spent the night there, and I expected our turn would come soon.

Like it or not, I was now an operational pilot, albeit one with pathetically little experience in both flying and operational flying. However, we were told that there would be another squadron "sweep" over France in the afternoon. I suppose, in a way, it is rather like waiting to see a dentist, only amplified, as life and limb were at risk. I managed to get in another session of practice flying, this time on my own, and I used the time to familiarise myself more with the aircraft and its behaviour in tight turns and the like.

Aerobatics were a delight and very different from the lighter and less powerful machines, where, for

His first operational Spitfire, AZ-A

instance, a loop was quite a tight circle.

In previous aircraft, you would perform a full-throttle climb to the top of the loop, then cut the throttle and pull back the stick, allowing the aircraft to whip over the top and come down. This machine was full throttle most of the way, and you powered the thing right around the circle. Quite different.

I had now amassed the princely total of fifty-odd flying hours, which, in hindsight, was laughable, but I was gaining confidence rapidly. Operation time came around all too soon, and twelve aircraft started up more or less simultaneously. We took off in twos, quickly formed up into the usual squadron formation, and turned onto our Southerly course.

We all selected channel "C" on the radio and, as I have said, maintained strict radio silence until the enemy was sighted. So, again, we concentrated on flying the tight formation until something happened. Whether we were being attacked or attacking, the word "Break!" would come over the radio. Our job, as number two, was to look after our number one until it was time to disperse. Then, it was a private battle for each and every one of us. The information would come over the radio, "Bandits, three o'clock high," or such directions.

I mentioned earlier that I was to experience an aircraft fault during this, my second operation, and it was as follows: Quite suddenly, the squadron broke into a melee of turns, dives, and climbs before I had any idea of what was happening. It wasn't long before I realised that my radio had packed up, and I pressed every button, hoping to get something out of it. But not a peep. In a matter of seconds, having not heard anything, I had no idea where I was, and what was more important, I had no idea where anyone else was either. I turned every way, but there wasn't a soul in sight. Now, the rule was that if your radio packed up, you came home, as it was deemed that unless you were in the middle of a scrap, you were not much use to anyone.

But this was only my second operation. How could I possibly turn homeward? That would be shameful. So I flew north, west, east, and south, climbed up a few thousand feet, and searched the skies. But there was nothing. What a dreadful position to be in. After a further five or ten minutes, I climbed high and weaved my way northwards. It is a basic rule of a fighter pilot to spend one-tenth of the time looking forward and nine-tenths looking in all directions - which I did in no uncertain terms.

I had been ensuring I would get home unmolested for so long that by the time I landed, the rest of the squadron was drinking tea in the dispersal. I say "the rest of the squadron," but that was not quite true. Three were missing- including my number one- Rover McLeod. This was a blow indeed. I reported shamefaced to the Commanding Officer and told him my tale. "Can't be helped," he said. "You did the right thing." - and that was that.

But it wasn't, was it? My mind was in turmoil. I felt that I had been of no use to anyone, especially the three who had not returned. I had not contributed whatsoever. I had to keep telling myself that it was not my fault, but it was little consolation.

The other pilots were full of stories, and two of them claimed a victory, as they had each shot down a Messerschmitt, and other pilots witnessed both. I had, however, gained some more vital experience, albeit very small. It is a fact that in this game, each day and each operation gave you more experience to help you return from the next day's operation.

Later that day, I was sent alone to do a convoy patrol. I picked up two ships somewhere off the Isle of Wight and escorted them along the south coast as far as Plymouth, where I was relieved of my duty by another Spitfire based in Cornwall. I waggled the wings to signal my departure, flew low and alongside the ships, and received a cheery wave from one of the crew. The convoy patrol allowed me to regain a little confidence and composure, and I reported back to the CO.

The next day, we were down to nine aircraft, and I was allocated a new number one. As a section, we were put on dawn readiness for the next morning. Nothing happened, and there was no "scramble."

Later that day, I was part of a section of four aircraft on a Rhubarb. This meant that the Leader (the Flight Commander) navigated, and we flew out across the Channel at nought feet or thereabouts. The intention was to attack a gun emplacement, which we did, and I do not doubt that we did a lot of damage. This was the first time I had fired the guns, and although there was return fire, I persisted until I had used up all my ammunition, and the four of us returned safely. The return fire, to say the least, was quite frightening. The Germans used tracer bullets about every tenth round, and it is a peculiar thing that each tracer seemed to be coming straight for you and veered off at the last second. But luckily, none of us was hit. We each made two or three attacks and then reformed, returning home.

The next few days were uneventful, and we were again made up to twelve by the arrival of three pilots and aircraft. One was a veteran, and the other two were beginners.

The next fighter sweep was a big affair with the whole Wing (3 squadrons) participating. We were briefed before takeoff by the Wing Commander, who ended his talk by saying: "To your horses, men!" What a fool, I thought. To me, it was no joke at all. He was a little chap (ex-Battle of Britain) who ended up in a grave in Tunisia - poor chap.

Some of the 234 Squadron, Ken is second from right

Again, as I shall relate, this operation proved disastrous for me. Someone, somewhere, was looking after me and continued to do so. This time, everything worked fine. The aircraft behaved beautifully - I was the one to cock it up!

Being such a large formation of thirty-six aircraft, the German radar picked us up, and as we crossed the French coast at about twenty thousand feet, we were very quickly engaged in an air battle, a dog fight as they were called. The squadron broke formation, and I clung to my number one. I must have been rather too conscientious in my duty that the first thing I saw in my mirror was the nose of a German fighter. He was so close that I could only see the engine and a little of his wings. His guns were blazing. I shall never know how he missed me. But miss me he did, and I quickly turned into a tight turn. One feature of the Spitfire was the ability to out-turn a 109 Messerschmitt, and this tight turn manoeuvre I had practised.

Let me explain that in a turn, when the wings of the aircraft are vertical, the controls are somewhat different. To increase the rate of turn, the stick is pulled back, and an up-and-down movement is accomplished by the rudder bar. However, in the turn, once you pull back on the stick to tighten the turn, the blood tends to leave the head and pile up in the legs. To lessen the effect, in a dogfight, the feet are placed on the top pedals of the rudder bar. Persistence in the turn makes the blood leave the eyes, and one cannot therefore see. This blindness results in unconsciousness, but with practice, one can release the stick slightly and remain conscious, albeit in a blacked-out state.

I did this and held the turn until I thought I had gotten him off my tail. I eased the stick forward; believe it or not, I was right on *his* tail. I madly pressed the gun button and pressed again and again. Hell! No guns! At that fateful second, he saw me and was quickly out of my sight. What on earth had happened, I thought. But not for long. I looked down and realised with horror that I had not moved the little lever to "FIRE". It was still on "SAFE". I was in a panic and cursed my stupidity.

I never got another chance, and the dogfight came to an end. We had both missed each other from close range, and afterwards, I thought he must have been as inexperienced as I was. Needless to say, I refrained from telling anyone about it. I should think that we had been attacked by a comparatively small section of aircraft that had one bash at us and then retired rather than face a larger force. Once again, I was not very proud of my efforts, and I began to think that my original intention of joining the RAF to be trained as a mechanic might have been a better idea. However, it was too late for such thoughts, and I must persist and do my very best. I don't recall the outcome of the day, but we lost two or three pilots and aircraft.

The next day, my Scottish friend was missing, and when I inquired about his whereabouts, I was told that he had reported sick. I never saw him again until after the war, but I was under the impression that he had decided it was too much for him to handle. He ended up as a Flight Controller in the Control Tower of some aerodrome or other. It's a great pity—but there you are.

Chapter 12

More of the Same Thing

The title of this chapter sums it up. The pattern of my life had been set, and the days were more or less the same, apart from some untoward events I shall write about.

The three Wing squadrons at Ibsley provided a Sector of two aircraft on readiness and a Sector on standby during all daylight hours from dawn to dusk. For the remainder of the time, the usual convoy patrols—Rhubarbs for specific targets across the Channel—and the usual fighter sweeps (either the squadron or the Wing) were every couple of days, depending mainly on how many aircraft and pilots were available.

We were typically high flyers in the true sense of the word - twenty thousand feet and above, so unless we were on a low-level operation of some sort, nought feet up to around eight thousand feet, we were not bothered much by flak, which is anti-aircraft fire from the ground. Being amidst that was a frightening experience, and if possible, one took evasive action to get out from under the curtain of exploding shells. As each shell exploded, there was a puff of grey-white smoke, and some were uncomfortably close. Although I was hit occasionally, it was of little consequence, thank God. Ibsley Airfield was never bombed, but places like Portsmouth, Southampton, and Plymouth got a hammering during the nighttime.

I only remember having two days off during my time at Ibsley, and I went with a friend on the bus to Bournemouth, where we did some shopping and visited a restaurant in the centre of town called Bobbys. I also visited Boots, the chemist, to buy throat paint and an angled brush. I occasionally suffered from a sore throat (tonsils), and this paint worked well. I also began to suffer from a persistent throat cough, which was entirely due to nerves and remained with me for a long time.

Ken, third from left

Losses of pilots and aircraft steadily mounted up, and one could not help wondering when it would be your turn. Air battles were indeed quite frequent, and I began to wonder if I would ever hit an enemy plane with my gunfire. The business of deflection shooting seemed beyond my grasp, and I will explain this in broad terms.

Imagine you are flying straight and level, and an enemy aircraft is approaching your line of flight at right angles to you from one side on a course ahead of you. When he crosses your line of fire, and you then shoot at him, by the time your bullets have reached the spot, he has moved on, and so, of course, you missed him. The idea, therefore, is to aim ahead of him so that your bullets will reach his line of flight when he gets there. This is a simple example of deflection shooting. The amount of deflection varies considerably, as you may imagine, with specific conditions. This is what I never seemed to be able to master. Remember, I had no gun firing practice when I arrived at the squadron. They say that practice makes perfect, but in my case, it did not.

The only practice I got was the real thing, and there was little chance of having another go at it. Attacking ground targets was a much simpler business, but the tendency here was to make repeated attacks until all the ammunition was used up. This, of course, was highly dangerous once alerting the ground defences, so a happy medium was always sought. Attacking aircraft and control towers on an enemy airfield caused lots of havoc, and you could see them grabbing any gun, even rifles and revolvers, and having a go at you. Combined with the usual anti-aircraft defences, these conveyed the message that we were not very welcome!

I shall now, as promised, relate the three events that were not part of the usual type of operation.

Firstly, I was scrambled (with one aircraft) one day and received my instructions from the Operations Room: Vector 130 degrees at Angels ten. It was regarding a balloon barrage. Balloon barrages were used for anti-aircraft defence; they were tethered to the ground with heavy cables and were designed to disrupt low-flying enemy aircraft, forcing them to fly higher and into the range of anti-aircraft guns. I was informed that one of the balloons was floating about, trailing its cable. I was told to destroy it. I found the balloon and used up all my ammunition, expecting it to burst into flames. But it did not; it just sank earthwards. Luckily, it drifted over the Channel, and I watched it hit the sea. I reported its position and returned to base.

Second story: We were told six aircraft would perform an air-to-ground attack with the Army on Salisbury Plain. The idea was for the Army to practice defences against a low, fast-flying attack against their equipment - in this case, half a dozen tanks. We were given an exact map reference, and we were to approach from a direction of our choice at nought feet. Our six aircraft attacked in line abreast over a rise in the ground so they would not see us coming. Any time during the afternoon, they said. Off we went and came over the rise and straight in - guns blazing. The sad part of this episode was that, although the tanks were actually wooden models and painted in camouflaged paintwork, the high-ranking Army Officers, who were the brains behind the event, parked their vehicles at one end, in line with the dummy tanks. The pilot on the left-hand side of our line abreast formation sighted his target - not a dummy tank but an Army vehicle containing spectators. Sadly, a Colonel was killed, and two or three Officers were wounded. The pilot was reprimanded, but it wasn't his fault, as we had only a few seconds to select a target and fire. No more was heard of the sad affair, but the spectators were well away from future Army cooperation exercises. I must say that all the dummy tanks were hit and were all but destroyed.

The third event was also a disaster, and I hesitate to relate it, but if one is writing down memories, then there is no point in not telling the truth. After all, this is not fiction.

MAKE IT DO

My number one, a Canadian called PO Cameron, and I were dispatched on a low-level reconnaissance to establish something or other on the coast of France. I don't remember exactly what we had to survey, but we came back with our report. On the way home, we saw above and ahead of us a flight of eight or nine aircraft, which we thought to be Messerschmitt 109s. After a minute or two, Cameron spoke to the Operations Room and was told that they were bandits. Therefore, we climbed and attacked from approximately 500 feet above and behind them. You have read my comment about deflection shooting; consequently, you will realise that the best way to shoot down an aircraft is from directly behind. Bear in mind that although we had a considerable (to me) number of operational flying hours under our belts, we were still amateurs at the game.

However, we attacked the trailing section, mine on the left and Cameron's on the right. Neither of us hit anything. In hindsight, we had opened up firing at too great a distance. So we climbed up and tried again. Unbelievably, they had still not seen us. On the second attack, Cameron hit his target and shot it down. I hit mine, but to no great extent, and it continued flying northwards. As I peeled off after my crummy attack, I saw RAF markings.

"They're Tomahawks!" I shouted over the radio. Oh hell, what an awful mess! We beat a hasty retreat and flew home, wondering what on earth we could say on our return. The Tomahawk is an American machine similar to the 109 Messerschmitt from certain angles. What could we do but tell the truth? We reported the disaster to the

Tomahawk plane, Ibsley

CO, who was furious. We later learned that the pilot bailed out of his Tomahawk and landed in the back garden of a house in Poole, near Bournemouth.

The next day, Cameron and I were instructed to fly to Group Headquarters, which I believe was located at an airfield called Colerne in the Bath and Bristol area. We were told to report to the Air Commodore in charge of 10 Group. Is this the end, we wondered?

We marched smartly into his office and saluted. He stared at us and then asked how many flying and operational hours we had. We told him. We then suffered an appalling dressing-down, and he concluded by saying that it is the duty of a fighter pilot to identify the target before opening fire. He said he had considered our lack of experience and would keep a close eye on us through our CO in case we encountered further troubles. We were ashamed of ourselves anyway and flew gloomily back to the squadron. Of course, everyone wanted to know all about it. Secretly - after it was all over - I said to myself: "Well, at least I've hit something" - although it was the wrong target. No more was heard about it, but within a few days, three unrelated things happened.

Firstly, the whole squadron was posted to RAF Portreath on the west coast of Cornwall, just north of St. Ives and quite close to the southern coast of Cornwall and Land's End. Secondly, Cameron was posted to a PRU Squadron somewhere. PRU means Photographic Reconnaissance Unit. These units were equipped with Spitfire Vs, stripped of armament, and carried extra fuel and cameras. They were used to photograph specific parts of France, Belgium, and other countries, and due to their reduced weight, they were appreciably faster. Thirdly, I was promoted to Flight Sergeant and appointed as a Section Leader!

Off we all went to Cornwall.

Chapter 13

Cornwall

It was now the beginning of May 1942.
The single runway at RAF Portreath ended at the edge of a cliff. The base also had a perimeter track, which served two main purposes: it housed a Fighter Wing, and it acted as the final staging post for aircraft heading to Gibraltar, Malta, and the Middle East. These departing planes were often old Wellington bombers, loaded with supplies bound for the Middle East Forces.

They were taken to the far end of the runway, which ran roughly east-west, with the prevailing wind being mostly west or southwest. Chocks were placed in front of their wheels, and when the pilot had completed all his checks, he opened the throttles to allow the engines to run as fast as possible. When the chocks were withdrawn, the aircraft trundled along the runway with all its weight, just about managing to get airborne by the time it reached the end of the runway. On the odd occasion, insufficient flying speed had been achieved, and the thing disappeared over the cliff edge, failing to manage lift and consequently ending up in the sea. Fortunately, these happenings were few and far between, but they happened on multiple occasions. Poor blokes. Some survived, and some did not. On the lighter side, there was one benefit to us. You have heard of the chap having a hearty breakfast before he was hanged. Well, these lads were given a glorious egg and bacon dinner the night before they took off, and we successfully joined them on many occasions.

I was lucky that one of the Women's Auxiliary Air Force waitresses in the Non-Commissioned Officers' Mess became a great friend of mine. For some unaccountable reason, she fell for me, so I could not go wrong. She was a pretty girl and would often stand at the kitchen door, waiting for us to arrive at meal times. As soon as she saw me, she would come running out of the kitchen with my meal, and much to the disgust of my compatriots, I was always served first. I, therefore, had little to no trouble obtaining the egg and bacon dinner, called a "Flap Supper." On one occasion, this young lady, as keen as ever to bring me my meal, literally ran from the kitchen but unfortunately tripped and spilt the meal all over my lap. I was compensated by receiving a larger meal than usual. I used to "chat her up" occasionally, but I cannot remember which part of the UK she came from. She gave me a photograph of herself and her two-year-old son! I said I would keep the picture, which I did, but I cannot remember what happened to it. Where her husband was, I know not, neither did I care.

After a couple of weeks in Portreath, we were down to eight pilots and aircraft and welcomed four new pilots and machines. One was an ex-Battle of Britain veteran named Ginger Lacey, who was famous at the time for his "KILLS", but he didn't stay long, only a couple of weeks. Perhaps he was sent as a morale booster. We also had a couple of Polish pilots who were - as Poles were - quick-tempered and very different from the British as they had an immense built-in hatred of the Germans and were so keen to get stuck in, that once airborne, they tended to disregard instructions and break formation on their own, as well as jam the radio with incessant jabbering in Polish, which wasn't a lot of use to the rest of us. Luckily, an all-Polish squadron was formed, and off they went to join their compatriots. We got a couple of Danish pilots who were also excellent.

We also had a visit from two personalities. One was Prince Bernhard of the Netherlands, who came to tell us what a good job we were doing! The other visitor was David Niven (or was that at Ibsley—I cannot remember). He was making a film called "The First Of The Few," which starred Leslie Howard, who played the part of the Spitfire designer, R. J. Mitchell. We appeared in the film in odd spots in a flying capacity.

RAF Portreath was subject to sudden periods of fog that never lasted more than 12 hours or so. One day, the squadron went on a low-level attack, and as we crossed the Channel and neared the UK coast, we encountered the fog. The CO ordered us to maintain the same height (or lack thereof), but I thought this was utterly stupid. Although I did as he said for a couple of minutes, I became convinced that it would end in disaster once we reached the coast. So I took my number two and climbed out of the fog. My action didn't receive punishment from the CO, as he sadly didn't survive. The result was that the leading four aircraft flew into the cliffs and were never seen again. What a shameful disaster! I landed with my number two at St Eval, a little way up the coast, refuelled, and waited for the fog to clear.

Let me explain the blind approach system, then in operation for use in fog, and compare it with the modern systems today. In the event of dense fog, we would be diverted to an adjacent airfield, but as happened quite often, by the time we returned from France, we did not have a great deal of petrol left out of the crummy 47 gallons. So, if it were at all possible, we would attempt to land at Portreath. One would make dirty darts at the leeward end of the runway and hope to see it when we got down to a few feet. To assist us was the "blind approach system" in the form of an airman who dashed out to the runway's end on his bike. He was armed with, believe it or not, a bike lamp and two pieces of coloured celluloid- one red and one green. He would stand there until he heard a Spitfire approaching and, in his infinite wisdom, would quickly decide whether we were too high or too low. If he thought we were OK, he would shine his bike lamp in our direction and put the requisite celluloid colour in front of it. As we were confronted with the usual problem of being unable to see forward on levelling out, it would be the last split second before we saw the lamp, or him, for that matter! It was hazardous, to say the least, but I never knew of anyone who was killed in this business, although there were more than a few pile-ups. So ends the story of the blind approach, which was conducted in the true meaning of the word "Blind".

Over the last few pages, I have concentrated on relaying the episodes and operations that were somewhat out of the ordinary, and I have more to come. But at this juncture, I must stress the importance and effects of day-to-day defensive and offensive operations on one's mind. Each operation was a hazardous and frightening experience that didn't seem to improve as time went on. There are a few pilots (and many aircrew for that matter) who had a reputation of being "brave", mainly because of their victories and the resultant fame and glory. In my opinion, for what it is worth, the brave airmen who had to steel themselves each time they took off and who persisted in pushing themselves to do as good a job as they were able to are the ones who should be congratulated - not the so-called "brave" who saw no fear whatsoever and stuck their necks out regardless of everyone around them and under their control. I make this remark not for self-praise, but because I believe it to be true. I have known such "brave" fighter pilots who became famous, but I refrain from mentioning their names.

There was a considerable difference between operating from the shores of the UK and operating in cooperation with the Army and virtually living close to the front line. In this respect, I take my hat off, and always will, to the PBI (in case you don't know - the Poor Bloody Infantry). The difference isn't extreme, but it is there.

Being based in the UK meant that one could return from an operation relatively quickly, and in the case of a fighter pilot, that meant comparatively short trips. Within, say, the space of one and a half to two hours, one had to get used to having cups of tea or a meal in the Mess and moments later fighting for one's life and then back to the safe airfield. One had to become somewhat of a schizophrenic and live two separate and distinctly different lives, but all in the same day.

The same life pertained on the front line (as I learned by becoming a front-line squadron member at the end of 1942). However, the schizophrenia tended to be somewhat diluted as when one landed after an operation, one was still very much in the firing line and suffered daily bombing of the airfield and artillery fire. If you can imagine, therefore, being in the air or on the ground became less of a schizophrenic lifestyle. I am sure anyone in this position during the Second World War would agree with me, especially those who operated in both spheres of war.

Chapter 14

Diversions From the Norm

It has been said many times since the Second World War that the Spitfire's design was remarkably excellent, and this is borne out by the many variants—or Marks—helping to maintain its position as a superb front-line fighting machine.

There were some twenty-five Marks altogether - all designed for a purpose. Some were high-flyers, some were low-level machines, some were faster than others, and some were designed to carry more fuel, thus extending their range. Some were clipped-wing models, some had wing tips strengthened, and had engines suitably modified to be faster at low levels and catch the infamous German V-1 rocket bomb launched against London from the shores of France. These chaps flew alongside the V-1 and nudged it off course by getting their reinforced wing tips under the wing of the V-1 and hopefully turning it back towards France. Apparently, they were quite successful. But the Mark Vs were the real workhorses of the war, and a few are still flying in a much quieter role today. This brings me nicely to the next story.

Four of us, being considered experienced pilots, were dispatched in our machines to Charmy Down airfield in the Bath and Bristol area. These cities had recently been suffering from night bombing raids, and some bright spark dreamt up the idea to make us guinea pigs.

We were to become night fighters! Whoever thought this one up should have been drummed out of the RAF - or, better still, given the job to do himself.

The established night fighter was an aircraft called the Boulton Paul Defiant. This was a single-engine machine, heavier than most, modified for night flying, with two crew members: the pilot and an air gunner who operated a rear-facing gun turret. To the best of my knowledge, very few of them were around in 1942. In fact, I do not recall ever seeing one. Their operation is self-evident, and they were equipped with the latest radar technology.

Ken, Centre back. 1942

However, the scheme at Charmy Down was as follows. They took a Boston Bomber (a twin-engine American aircraft with a crew of four), cut the nose off of it, and replaced it with a searchlight. With radar and help from the ground, they would seek out enemy night bombers. A Spitfire would fly slightly behind, above, and to one side of the Boston, maintaining radio contact with it. Having positioned itself behind the enemy, the Boston would get as close as possible and switch on the searchlight. Down we would come and attack. The Boston would remain there, illuminating the enemy until they saw the Spitfire pass them, and then they would veer to one side, leaving us to finish the job.

Imagine, if you can, the situation we found ourselves in. Firstly, the potentially vicious swing on takeoff can be problematic even for experienced pilots. Secondly, the exceptionally narrow undercarriage made night landing a hazard. Lastly, the lack of forward vision during takeoff and landing, along with the glow surrounding the red and white hot exhaust stubs, made life difficult.

Having the exalted rank of Flight Sergeant - the other three were Sergeants - I was in charge of the fighter element of the unit. I ensured, for obvious reasons, that we all had the same number of sorties, which typically numbered two or three per night, depending on the frequency of bombing raids. The result of this incredible exercise was no enemy bombers shot down, but an unnecessary loss of two of our team. These losses occurred on takeoff and landing. After about 10 days, the higher-ups decided to abort the exercise, and the remaining two of us thankfully flew back to Portreath to a job we knew more about: Daylight flying. Bye-bye, Charmy Down.

On a practice flight shortly after this, I was again testing the limits of my Spitfire, and it was a valuable experience for future use. However, on this occasion, I decided to establish just how fast the plane would go. I took it up to twenty-odd thousand feet when it was beginning to waffle about a bit in the rarefied atmosphere. I turned it on its back, stuck the nose vertically downwards, opened the throttle, and watched the airspeed indicator. I cannot remember the exact figure on the clock, but when I computed it for height, it was well over 450 m.p.h.! Getting a bit scared, I pulled it out of the dive. All was well until I came to the landing. Upon approaching the airfield, the plane was flyable, but it was behaving in a peculiar fashion. When I got out, I walked around it and eventually noticed that the tailplane was no longer horizontal and the fin no longer vertical. Rather shamefacedly, I reported my actions, and the machine was grounded.

Within a day or two, representatives from the Supermarine factory arrived in bowler hats and examined the machine. They were rather perplexed and dismayed, and arranged to transport my plane back to the factory. I was quite upset to lose my "AZ-A" after all this time, but it was entirely my fault. The incident caused

Ken's "AZ-A"

great interest in the squadron, but luckily for me, there was no reprimand.

Sometime later, I was on readiness when the call came through: "Scramble one aircraft!" - off I went and was told Vector and Angels instructions. They said the cloud base was around 500 feet, so it was, and I went into the cloud. I never liked cloud flying, but there was one important rule. You must always, *always*, believe your instruments. I did this implicitly. They will tell you the truth when your mind will not. You sometimes feel that you are climbing or diving or have one wing low, but your instruments say no. I stayed on the course and climbed at the specified speed- and I climbed, and climbed, and climbed. Should I turn back or not? I plodded on and up, however, and at just over 20 thousand feet, I came out of the cloud. Thank God.

I reported, "Angels 21—quilt." This word conveyed to them that I was just above the cloud, not a soul in sight. After a minute or two, the message came: "Return to base." I cursed under my breath and then had to face the downward flight through thick clouds. "Instruments, instruments," I thought, and plunged in. I got back safely and told the tale on landing. It was not a very nice trip.

June arrived, and the squadron was instructed to pack our small kit and fly to Tangmere, near Chichester. No reason was given for the operation, but we found ourselves patrolling the French coast the next day. We were, of course, as usual, the top cover. We patrolled from early morning, returned, refuelled, and patrolled most of the day. What were we patrolling for, we wondered, and it was not until a couple of days later that we heard the reason. Until now, the Army Units had not had anything to do since Dunkirk except train and train. We discovered this event was a trial invasion of Dieppe*, which ended in complete disaster. Many Canadians were killed and many taken prisoner in the abortive attempt to succeed in the mission.

When we returned to Portreath, we conducted another similar exercise, operating for a day or two from an airfield near Chichester. This was due to the German "Scharnhorst" battleship making a run through the English Channel. I understand that the Fleet Air Arm made contact and launched some of their torpedoes, but we never saw them. The weather was very poor, and again we missed out. There must have been a lot of aeroplanes flying about in bad weather, and it is a wonder that there were no mid-air crashes. But perhaps there were.

Back at Portreath, there had been a series of hit-and-run daylight German raids on the south coast of Cornwall. These raiders were coming across at a low level (just as we did), and the radar would not

---

* The Dieppe Raid (19 August 1942) was an Allied amphibious assault on the German-occupied French port of Dieppe. Intended as a test for future landings, the raid was a disaster: of nearly 6,000 troops—mostly Canadian—over 3,300 were killed, wounded, or captured. The lessons learned later informed the planning of D-Day.

pick them up until it was almost too late. To combat this, a section of two aircraft was dispatched from Portreath precisely at dawn when there was sufficient light to take off. We flew to a field, and I mean a plain field, on the Lizard Point. There, we landed, turned into the wind, and sat in our planes with the radio switched on. We were scrambled as soon as the Ops Room radar picked up the raiders. We immediately took off and gave chase. After takeoff from the field, we were replaced by another two aircraft. Although this system continued for some time, I never heard of any success, and eventually, the scheme was abandoned.

One new member of the squadron was an ex-Battle of Britain pilot named Drinkwater. I shall never forget his name. Very unusual indeed. I was chatting to him one day and happened to mention that I could do with a spot of leave. "Forget it," he said. "Going on leave is great, but coming back to this is awful. You are much better off staying put. Not that I recall ever getting any leave anyway."

I had heard of an outfit called MSFU, which means Merchant Ship Fighter Unit, and as I felt I was due for a change, I applied for a posting. I will say here and now that I heard no more about it, and in hindsight, I was rather glad. The Merchant Ship convoys plying between the UK, Canada, and America were, on occasion, attacked by a long-range German Bomber called a Condor. These aircraft sought out convoys, attacked with bombs, and beat a hasty retreat - quite sensibly. If they had no bombs left, there was no point in hanging about, especially if they were getting out of their range. To combat this, one of the Merchant Ships would be fitted with a catapult of some sort, which carried a clapped-out old Hurricane, which was just about on its last legs. Two pilots were on board, each standing on readiness for half the daylight hours. On being scrambled, the Hurricane would be catapulted off in an attempt to shoot down the Condor.

There was no provision for landing back on, so the idea was to judge the wind direction and bail out so as to land in the sea in front and to one side of the convoy. The destroyer patrolling the convoy would then pick up the pilot from his watery position. There was a significant issue: if the pilot misjudged the situation and landed in the sea in the wrong position, the destroyer would not turn back to rescue him. You can see why I was pleased not to hear any more about the posting. The same system was applied to the convoys to Russia, but I was told that after more than two and a half minutes in the ice-cold sea, there was little hope of survival.

Around mid-July, the CO sent for me, and on the way to his office, I wondered what the hell I had done now. "Report to the Air Officer Commanding 10 Group at Colerne tomorrow at 10:00 am," he said. "Was this more trouble?" I thought. I looked at him, and with a smile, he said, "I have put you up for a Commission. Best of luck!" Yes, Sir," I said and came out feeling quite elated!

The business of rank was somewhat of a farce, especially in fighters with a one-man crew. As a Flight Sergeant, I had on numerous occasions led the flight, which, according to the rules, was the job of a Flight Lieutenant. I understand that later in the war, an Aircrew Mess was brought in rather than an Officers' Mess or a Non-Commissioned Officers' (NCO) Mess. This was a much better idea, as some NCO pilots, including Sergeants, Flight Sergeants, and Warrant Officers, refused Commissions for reasons best known to themselves.

However, I arrived at 10 Group Headquarters and found I was one of about a dozen pilots from various squadrons in the Group. We were given forms to fill out with details of our education, flying hours, operational flying hours, and the squadron we served in. I filled in my form but refrained from answering one question: "What was your father's job or profession?" I didn't see how that related to my capabilities as a pilot or leader of pilots.

The first lad for the interview came out and said to all of us, "I don't stand a bloody chance—my old man is a Welsh Miner!" I don't know whether he was successful.

However, the Air Commodore, I believe, told me in no uncertain terms that if I was asked a question, I had to answer it. Apart from that, the interview went along quite smoothly, and I flew back to Portreath. It will take some time for me to fully incorporate the outcome of this interview into my story.

At the beginning of August, the squadron was ordered to fly up to Biggin Hill in Kent, and we were expected to stay there for some time. Fierce air battles were taking place over the Channel and the coast of France, particularly around Calais, and they sought to amass as many fighters as possible. When we got there, we realised they were right – there *really* were some air battles going on! Also, the daylight bombing raids had started. The Americans took most of the daylight raids, and the British saw to the night bombing raids.

Our first job was to escort some American B-29 Superfortresses on a raid of an industrial target. Due to our limited range, we could only escort them so far and then return home. Then we would go out again as far as we could and escort them back to the UK. I remember once, upon escorting them back, that one of the Fortresses had been badly hit by anti-aircraft fire, and the rear gunner was wounded. We were, of course, on the same radio wavelength, so I heard all that was happening inside the Fortress. The rear gunner, on the bottom of the fuselage, found it impossible to rotate his turret to get out of it, so he was stuck there. The hydraulics had been hit, so the pilot said he would have to belly-land the machine as he could not lower his wheels. The poor rear gunner could hear all this and knew he was destined to be squashed on landing. I have never forgotten it—the poor chap.

I was involved in a scrap over Calais shortly after. My plane was hit, but not severely enough to cause significant damage. In the ensuing melee, I did a violent manoeuvre requiring quick and heavy use of the rudder bar. My foot shot off the top pedal and somehow wedged between the top and bottom footrest. The pain was quite severe as I had wrenched my foot and toes sharply backwards. I landed with my foot still through the gap. On landing, I said to the fitter, "You will have to help me out of this thing." It took some time to extricate my foot, and he helped me to stumble back to the dispersal hut.

I was carted off to Orpington Hospital, but at least I had shot a lump off a ME-109. Because of my foot trouble, I did not see him bail out or go down. I was credited with a "DAMAGED" – wonderful!

The hospital diagnosed traumatic synovitis and said I would have to have a short-wave treatment. The foot and ankle were bandaged into a metal cover and taken out only during treatment sessions. And so it came to pass – as they say – that I spent my 21st birthday in hospital. I stayed there for about 10 days, then returned to Biggin Hill, where I found my plane, which had been patched up. There was nothing more serious than bullet holes.

I flew back to Portreath and rejoined the squadron. There were three incidents from that August that spring to mind. I was, and had been for some considerable time, the "oldest inhabitant" of the squadron.

Such were the losses of pilots, and I thanked my lucky stars that I was still around and prayed that my good luck would hold, as indeed it did. I had still not succumbed to alcohol. I still had not had the good sense to resort to alcohol to alleviate the strain and pressures of life on a squadron. I was not the only abstainer; there were others, but I must admit they were rather few and far between. Operations still frightened the life out of me, but I will say in my defence, so to speak, that I never flunked a duty and always gave my best. My record of "KILLS" shows that this was not very good, but that's how it was.

Again, I do not recall much time off—I visited the town of Redruth one afternoon, but no other trips spring to mind. I never even got as far as Portreath village, and I never knew the location of our Ground Control, or Ops Room, as they called it. It was not until many years later that my son, David, visited Portreath village and discovered that the Ops Room had been turned into a bar and was now called such.

A select few of us had a flight to Colerne to view a Focke-Wulf 190, a German fighter. This was their newest fighter and was rather superior to the ME-109. It was presumed that the pilot had lost his bearings and was flying south when he crossed the Bristol Channel and, mistaking it for the English Channel, landed at the first airfield he saw. When he stepped out of his 190, he closed the hood and told those who immediately surrounded him that if anyone opened the hood, the plane would explode. This kept them guessing for a time, but eventually, they opened it up. We had a good, close look at it, which was very informative, as these 190s were our new opponents. The pilot was, of course, taken prisoner.

Incident number two was one that left us all deeply shaken. Not far up the Cornish coast was the airfield at Saint Eval. One night, a German aircraft dropped a land mine by parachute, and it fell directly onto an air-raid shelter. Tragically, nearly a dozen members of the Women's Auxiliary Air Force were killed.

The third incident concerns a Rhubarb by two aircraft - my number two and I. As we were leaving France, flying very low, I spotted a ship near the French coast. It seemed to be a converted merchant ship of some sort and was obviously German. I climbed up about five hundred feet and attacked it. We both made two runs at it, and we could see we had hit it. Unfortunately, on the second run-in, my number two was hit.

The mass of return fire convinced me that it was, in fact, a flak ship*, and the barrage was frightening indeed. We turned northwards, and my number two said he was losing height. He did his best to keep the thing in the air, but eventually had to get out of it. I circled around him, immediately changed to channel "D" on the radio, and called "Mayday, Mayday." The code word "Mayday" originated from the French "m'aider," which means "help me." I got an immediate response and was told to transmit for 20/30 seconds whilst they got a "fix" on me. I kept circling around the pilot as he got into a dinghy. I stayed with him as long as my fuel would permit, but before I left, I transmitted again for them to check the position. I went low past him, and he waved. He was OK, and I waved back. The Air Sea Rescue boys picked him up, and he was back in the squadron a few days later. Excellent work by the Air Sea Rescue, who always went to great lengths to rescue airmen, even within sight of the enemy coast.

Sometime during September, I was posted to RAF Digby, in Lincolnshire, to 242 Squadron. I went by train to Digby and, after reporting, found that there were pilots from other squadrons and Ground Crews from all over the place.

On leaving Portreath, I said farewell to the squadron and my faithful fitter and was very sorry to lose him. He was a very conscientious chap and was always interested in my operations. The only time I annoyed him was when I brought "AZ-A" back with a twisted fuselage. However, I was now to move on.

But to end this chapter on "Diversions from the norm," I will write about a very pleasant task that fell my way a couple of times. On odd occasions, we had the pleasure of hosting members of the area Air Training Corps (ATC). Like its counterparts, the Sea Cadets and Army Cadets, it comprised young persons, mainly boys in those days, who were interested in a particular branch of the Services.

On the appointed day, they would march from the Main Gate of the aerodrome to our dispersal site under the command of their officer. Depending on their number, they would be split into small groups of three or four. They would then be handed over to us, and we would take

---

* A flak ship was a heavily armed vessel, often converted from a merchant ship, equipped with anti-aircraft guns designed to shoot down enemy aircraft.

them on a tour of the squadron area, explaining everything to them. They were all very keen and asked dozens of questions. The climax of the tour, of course, was the aeroplane itself - the Spitfire. A considerable amount of time was spent showing them everything about it and letting them, one by one, sit in the cockpit, where all the instruments, knobs, levers, and other controls were explained. Again, a multitude of questions. The final stage of the tour was a trip in an aeroplane, and for this purpose, we used the faithful Tiger Moth with its two cockpits. Again, a short description of the instruments and controls. Then, a flight. They were strapped in, given a helmet and goggles, and connected to the speaking tube. The mixture of apprehension and delight on their faces was incredible to behold. A short trip of about fifteen to twenty minutes was given to each in turn. Although it was forbidden, I would demonstrate the effects of using the control column (or joystick as it was once called) and then let them have a go themselves. You can imagine the delight, especially when they related their experience to other lads on landing. It was, therefore, highly pleasurable to us. I do not know how much the occasions affected the careers of the lads involved, although I would imagine that quite a high percentage of them eventually joined the RAF.

Chapter 15

Embarkation and Disembarkation

The RAF Station at Digby in Lincolnshire was heaving with personnel. The pilots were all Spitfire lads, and after booking in, we just hung about.

Why were we here? What was going on? A multitude of questions, but no single answer. There were no aircraft for us, and everyone was guessing. The secrecy surrounding the affair was absolute and one hundred per cent. After a few days, we were given embarkation leave and issued with railway warrants to our chosen destinations. We had to take all our kit and were instructed to lighten the load somewhat. Leave at last, I thought, but it had the word embarkation in front of it, which made a difference. We were allowed four days at home, which was great, but it flew by.

I reported back to Digby, but there was still no news of our future. I had not heard anything about my commission and concluded that failing to answer the question about my father had perhaps branded me with insubordination in front of the Air Commodore. On my return, I met a Sergeant Pilot who hailed from Exmouth, and we became good friends. Believe it or not, he was another Ken. After a day or two, we were issued a fur coat, fur gloves, and a fur hat. "Good God, it's Russia!" We thought. Two days later, we were told to hand in our fur clothing, and the next day, we were issued a Tropical Kit. What a mad-house! From top to bottom, ranks got their orders for the day, and the secrecy remained absolute. Nobody knew what on earth was going on. And that state of affairs would remain so for some time to come.

242 Squadron ready to depart. But where to? Ken, far right.

They left us with our tropical kit, and after another couple of days, we were marshalled and taken to a railway station. We were instructed to ensure our water bottles were full, and then we boarded a train. The carriages were old-fashioned, i.e., without a corridor, and as each compartment filled, it was locked. This was indeed very strange, but it was obviously intended to maintain secrecy. The train soon started and chuntered through the evening and night. I may say, at this point, that in those wartime days, all station names had been obliterated, as had all road signposts, so we had no means of establishing our whereabouts. The next morning, we came to a halt and soon established that we were in Gourock on the Clyde.

There were ships of all sizes anchored in the estuary and many ferry-crafts, all with numbers. We were each given a chit showing our ferry number, and we waited in turn. Even the most unintelligent could fathom that we were in for a sea voyage. My time at sea was minimal.

MAKE IT DO

One voyage from Fleetwood to the Isle of Man and another to Belfast in Northern Ireland was my sum total, but that had been enough to show me that I was no sailor. Bobbing up and down in a boat was not my idea of fun or even enjoyment. I considered the problem, and upon examining the array of crafts, I realised that the best chance for me was to make the largest ship. I suggested to my friend that we might be better off on a liner. The first step was to determine which ferry would take us to the ocean liner. This was easily done, and we disposed of our chits for the correct ferry. My friend was in complete agreement with the scheme, and we soon found our way onto the ferry of our choice and were taken out to a twenty-one thousand-ton liner called the "Stratheden". This was very naughty, and as punishment, we arrived after twelve days at sea in the wrong place at the wrong time. This story will show what happened to us and what should have happened.

The liner had been converted from a cruise ship to a troop ship, and bunks and hammocks were everywhere. Very few RAF personnel were aboard, and most passengers were Army. The total number of personnel carried was some 5,500. It was an enormous convoy. I have heard that up to 700 ships were involved. We set sail quite quickly on October 27th, and the secrecy remained. I was told that even the Captain did not know the destination, but opened his orders daily. Rumours, of course, were rife, and we learned that at one time, we were two days out of New York. True or false - I do not know. It was quite miserable on board, and we spent a lot of time on deck trying to ease the seasickness. However, all things come to an end, and we eventually made landfall. On our final day onboard, we were given a lecture. This was the scheme - at long last.

Montgomery and his Desert Rats had been struggling to advance westwards along the coast of North Africa, where many battles were fought against the Germans and Italians. Places like Tobruk, El Alamein, Benghazi, etc., are now famous battle sites, and the front line moved backwards and forwards from Egypt and the Canal Zone. The idea then was plain to see. Allied forces would invade Algeria in western North Africa. They would fight their way eastwards into Tunisia and, hopefully, meet the Eighth Army and the Desert Rats, thus driving the Germans and Italians out of North Africa, so that the war against Germany could be launched on the European mainland.

And so we landed in Algiers on November 8th or 9th. The other recruited pilots of 242 and other squadrons obeyed the rules and were shipped from Gourock straight to Gibraltar by Destroyers, where Spitfires had arrived in crates from the UK and were readily assembled. They then flew across to Algiers at the appointed invasion time and landed at Maison Blanche airfield. At the same time, American forces had landed at Oran and on Morocco's coast.

This is what we were about. The American 1st Army and some Units of the American Air Force joined the British and Commonwealth forces at our western end. It is somewhat remiss of me not to mention the Navy and Fleet Air Arm, and I now do so, but I know little of their movements.

Ken and I felt rather like waifs and strays when we disembarked, but we soon established the whereabouts of our squadron. It served us right, I suppose, that we had to walk, with our kit, from the harbour at Algiers to Maison Blanche airport, but we did, and we got extremely hot in the process. We arrived at the airport long last, only to find that the squadron had moved on and flown eastwards to Setif. We felt somewhat deserted, but of course, it was entirely our fault, or should I say more truthfully, my fault. Not to worry, we thought, Spitfires were being flown in frequently from Gibraltar and were parked all over the place, including alongside the runway. We checked one or two and found that they had been refuelled. We sought out the RAF Stores officer and informed him that we were late arrivals for 242 Squadron, but had been put on the wrong ship in the UK and had arrived in Algiers instead of Gibraltar.

The story was believed without question, and we asked permission to take a couple of Spitfires and fly east to join our squadron. A reasonable request, we thought. He flatly refused. "Then how do we get out of here?" we said. "Perhaps the Army can help," he replied, and off we went to search for someone. We found him - an Army Captain, and told him our plight. "Can we get a lift?" we asked. "I'll do better than that," he said. "I have plenty of vehicles that have arrived by sea, but no drivers. So, the sooner I get them into the front line, the better. Can you drive?" "Yes," we said. "Right," he said, "out there are several three-ton Bedford trucks with trailers. Take one up to the front line and deliver it." We threw in our kit and set off. There was plenty of spare petrol in cans, and off we went. We had changed our profession somewhat, but I supposed it was all for a good cause - or was it?

We drove eastward and headed for the squadron at a small town called Setif. The length of the journey has disappeared in the mists of time, but sometime later, we came to the mountains. These were the Saharan Atlas Mountains, and the road deteriorated. It wound up the mountainside for ages, and we had to reverse on some of the bends more than once. With the caravan trailer behind, this was not easy—or at least not for us.

We found it impossible to get both the lorry and the trailer around one particular corner. We stopped and had a powwow. We had to proceed somehow or other and didn't intend to start walking. The trailer was practically on the precipitous edge of the road. We agreed upon the solution, and having unhooked the trailer, one of us gave it a nudge with the back end of the lorry. It was a fascinating sight to see it somersaulting down the mountainside. Eventually, it burst open, and hundreds of papers took to the air. What papers, we wondered. It was obviously some administration trailer or perhaps an Orderly Room. Our problem was solved. But this was war, we thought, and funny things happen in a war. It was sort of difficult to say exactly whose side we were on at that time. Therefore, I request that the reader maintain a certain level of respectful discretion regarding such events. I am still alive, and the arm of the law is long.

We arrived in Setif and, fortunately, found the correct Army Unit very easily, where we traded our Bedford 3-tonner for a lift to the airfield, where the squadron was stationed.

We reported to the CO and gave him the exact string of lies about how we had the misfortune of being ferried to the wrong ship in Gourock. We were welcomed anyway, as they had already lost pilots and planes. We told him all about the lines of Spitfires on Maison Blanche airfield, and how we had been unable to get two without the requisite chit. We informed the CO of our journey from Algiers, and his response was astounding. I don't recall his exact words, but this is how it went. "You seem to be quite capable of getting from A to B," he said. "Go back to Maison Blanche and bring back two Spitfires. If you are successful, I'll send someone else as well." We were nonplussed, to say the least.

Nevertheless, we took just our small kit and made our way down the main road, thinking we should get a lift. In a war zone, Army traffic constantly buzzes back and forth to the front line. But somehow, we were unlucky and didn't come across anyone going the full distance to Algiers.

But we did come across something! It was a quite nice saloon car, obviously belonging to a civilian, as there were no Army markings on it whatsoever. And the ignition key was in it. The phrase "All is fair in love and war" came to mind again, and we got into it and drove westward. We scrounged petrol here and there from the Army, but I think some of it had an octane value not particularly liked by the engine. However, it chuntered on, and we felt we should not stop it - even for a night's rest. So we took turns driving through the night. As far as I recall, we had only one night to suffer on the trip, and eventually, we arrived at Maison Blanche aerodrome with the engine behaving rather badly. We parked it and sloped off to plan our campaign. We first checked on the Spitfires' availability, and they were still there. We again approached the Stores officer and told him that the CO of 242 Squadron had sent us back to obtain replacement Spitfires. The answer was the same as before: no chit, no aircraft. So we arranged for a bed for the night. During our wait, we discovered that "our" motor car had belonged to an Official of the town of Algiers and had been given to the Group Captain in charge of Maison Blanche. Some dirty dog had pinched it and driven it eastwards to Setif, where we found it. Fancy that! The Group Captain was pleased indeed to retrieve his motor, but not very pleased when the engine would not start. In hindsight, I would say that it was suffering from valve trouble.

We were ready by dawn, and our plan was quite simple. We would walk out across the aerodrome and take the two Spitfires furthest away from H.Q. We had brought our parachutes, and as we set off to walk, we noticed several small yellow objects which seemed to have little metal wings. Luckily, we avoided them and found out later that they were antipersonnel bombs, which had been dropped by a German raider the previous night. Fortunately, there were none on the runway. Apart from that, it was straightforward to reach our objective, and we took off, returning to the landing strip at Setif the same day, as they say in the Air Force: Duty Carried Out.

MAKE IT DO

A point of interest that comes to mind relatively late is that the convoy that brought us out from the UK also had two sister liners to the "Stratheden". These were the "Strathmore" and the "Strathavon". On their return journey to the UK, when, of course, the German U-boats had become aware of what was now going on in this new theatre of war, two of these three sister ships were torpedoed and sunk. C'est la Guerre!

Chapter 16

The Campaign Called "Torch"

Some could argue that I had been on a holiday since leaving Portreath. Call it what you will, but I was certainly back in the war now, and it started by getting to know all the pilots of the squadron. The squadron was composed of pilots from various Spitfire squadrons throughout the United Kingdom. The aircraft were unchanged Mark Vs, except that the centre carburettor air intake had been moved further forward, up to the nose of the plane, to a position very close to the propeller, and fitted with a finer filter. This was to combat swirling sand and heat.

I recall places in Algeria and Tunisia that will be mentioned in the stories, including Philippeville (now called Skikda), Annaba (formerly Bône), Sétif, Constantine, Djelfa, Medjez El Bab, Jendouba (also known as Souk El Arba), Le Kef, Bizerte, Tunis, and Sfax, among others.

From Bône and all points eastward, we operated from landing strips instead of grass airfields or runways. This was the system from now on. As the Army moved forward, a site would be selected by the Army Engineers, who would then bulldoze a strip of land and level it as much as possible. Then, a metal-linked runway would be laid. One type (which I took to be British) consisted of firm, open wire netting, reinforced every foot or so with heavy steel rods. The American type was called "Sommerfield Track" and was made of solid but perforated steel sheets that interlocked with each other. Both types made a runway about 12 feet wide. They served the purpose very well, but one had to be careful of pools of water collecting after nightly heavy rainstorms. On takeoff, if one hit one of these pools, it tended to slow the aircraft and push the nose down momentarily, so vigilance was the key. However, that was the system, and a landing strip could be laid down in a remarkably short time, and the Army then moved on to the next job, wherever and whenever that may be. Supplies of petrol and shells for the guns were also dumped there.

Operation Torch landings

We arrived back at Setif only to find that the squadron had moved on. This was incredible and somewhat upsetting. We considered that we had done a pretty good job and deserved a break. As we were temporarily our bosses, we decided to check out the town of Setif. We wandered down the main street, like tourists, and looked around. I mention this because the visit taught us something about life that we had hitherto not encountered.

The sign outside the building read 'Cafe-Bar,' so in we went. At some point, we had drawn some pay via our pay books. This, again, was something new. Our pay was in British Military Money and comprised one-pound, ten-shilling, and one-shilling notes. These were, of course, as new to the Algerians as they were to us. However, we had little difficulty using them and went into the cafe bar. It was a medium-sized two-storey building, and the ground floor was as one would expect, with a bar at one end and tables and chairs. On three sides, there was an indoor balcony with approximately a dozen rooms leading off it. We ordered two coffees and surveyed the scene. There was a staircase to the balcony in two corners of the room, and a queue of Army lads at the bottom of each stairway. At regular intervals, a young lady (and some of them not so young) would emerge from an upstairs room, escort a soldier down the stairs, offer him a farewell, and take the next man's hand in the queue. We watched with great interest and realised we had stumbled across a brothel.

To say that we were naive would, of course, be true. We had received a certain amount of training in the art of flying an aeroplane and using it as a weapon of war, but had not received much education about the outside world, especially life in its raw form. Two things came to mind. Firstly, the lectures at Babbacombe regarding venereal disease and my Mother's farewell command about keeping away from girls wearing grass skirts! So this was, to some extent, what it was all about. We ordered another coffee and were visited at our table by the "Madam," who spoke, as they all did, in French. The gist of the conversation was an invitation to be introduced to one or two of the young ladies. Some were French Algerians, and others were Arabs. However, I can say in all truthfulness that we declined her invitation. In hindsight, one must remember that the lads partaking of the pleasures available did not know how long they had to live, so they were game for anything. We returned to the airstrip, chatting about our adventure.

The squadron had moved on to a town and port on the coast called Bône, so we went there, trusting that we would be able to remain with the squadron at long last and get on with our jobs.

We reported to the CO, who congratulated us and examined the two Spitfires. He informed me that the plane I had now delivered was henceforth his machine, and he showed me the one I was to have. I grumbled a bit as my new plane had only flown from Gibraltar to Algiers and from there to Bône. It was virtually brand new. The one he gave me already appeared to be suffering somewhat from its use, but he was a Squadron Leader, and I was a mere flight sergeant. So there was no argument.

The Allied Forces had advanced rapidly eastwards, although the Germans were already offering some resistance, which increased as the days passed. The squadron, which had started with sixteen pilots and machines, was already down to about nine or ten, so things hadn't been all that easy. It was obvious that as we advanced from the west and the desert lot advanced from the east, the enemy forces were gradually being compressed into a smaller area and were not giving up easily.

We were straight into the war once again. The airfield at Bône was quite close to the town and harbour, so we began to suffer night bombing raids as well as our daytime offensives. Ground crews were often in short supply, as we quickly adapted ourselves to refuelling and rearming our machines. Petrol was shipped out from the UK in relatively fragile tins, which, if I recall, held about five gallons. I did not know why, but a fair quantity of these petrol tins contained tiny amounts of water. Some said it was sabotage, maybe it was, but I rather doubted it. However, as most people will know, it does not take much water at all in a carburettor, or elsewhere in the fuel system for that matter, to stop an engine or at least produce erratic performance - both of which in a single engine machine are, to say the least, disastrous. So an urgent order to the UK quickly resolved the problem; they, whoever they were, dispatched a load of chamois leathers to the Fighter Squadrons together with some large funnels. Every time we filled our planes with petrol, we did so via a chamois leather stuffed into a funnel. Problem solved. Eventually, the supplies of petrol were uncontaminated, and the filtering ceased.

The operations in the air were the same as ever, except that there were more of them. We were very busy with offensive sweeps into enemy territory, air battles, reconnaissance for the Army, air-to-ground targets, etc. So, to obviate the reader's boredom, I shall confine my writings to events that were out of the norm and that I trust will provide interesting reading. As Non-Commissioned Officer pilots, we were accommodated in bell-tents, six or so to a tent, and there was a Cook's tent, but I do not recall a "Mess" as such, so we probably got our grub and ate it in our own tent. The food was, to say the least, boring and consisted mainly of "K" rations - sometimes called Compo-rations. Lots of corned beef and tough biscuits.

Having said that, our Squadron Cook was somewhat of a wizard in the kitchen. He was an effeminate man who, according to rumour, was a one-time Assistant Chef at the Savoy Hotel in London. I remember his name well. He was excellent once he got used to his monotonous supplies, and I did hear that his prowess reached far and wide and that he ended up as batman-cook to Field Marshal Montgomery. I don't know how true that was, but he certainly was good! The Arabs would come and sell us eggs, which greatly supplemented our diet. They seemed to be quite oblivious to the war going on around them and were very friendly. Nevertheless, our stores of every description were well and truly guarded all day and night. There was also a certain amount of fraternisation with the local French people in and around the town of Bône, and this brings me to say a little about two personalities on the squadron. These two were completely different in all aspects, except one.

Firstly, there was our Cypher Sergeant, who was, of course, a non-flyer and was really dirty and scruffy. The other was a Sergeant Pilot. However, the thing they had in common was a peculiarity of nature, which I had certainly never met before and very seldom since. They had a magical effect on the opposite sex. Women were absolutely besotted and defenceless against them, even from the first eye contact. It had nothing to do with their good looks, their smart dress, or anything else like that. It was indeed a quirk of nature and positively incredible.

The Cypher Sergeant, as I have said, was a dirty, loathsome individual who never seemed to wash and who ate like a pig. I was told that, before the war, he was one of the editors of a journal called "The English Digest". However, as Senior NCO Pilot, I had to warn the chap that unless he improved his habits, I would have no alternative but to tell him to leave the "Mess" and fend for himself. In my ignorance, I thought this would scare him into action, but it didn't in the slightest. Although he always turned up for his cypher duties, he would often go off into town to seek accommodation and food. He found these without trouble and was fed and housed by the ladies of the local brothel! I was amazed, but his mystical powers came into action, catering to his requirements.

The Sergeant Pilot was a good lad who, whilst in the UK, had nine pregnant young ladies after him. So, he desperately applied for an immediate posting overseas, and the powers that be looked kindly on his predicament; thus, he joined us. Again, his exploits in the town were incredible, and what is more, I genuinely believed him. "If you require proof of what I've told you," he would say, "then you must come with me." I declined the offer. These two fellows had a quality (if that is the word) that a high percentage of the male population may well welcome.

The sad endings of these two stories are that the CO got the cypher chap posted somewhere and was never seen again. The pilot was shot down and killed during our stay at Bône.

I was returning one day from a lone operation and was flying towards Bône along the coast when I spotted a craft travelling at what appeared to be high speed towards Bône. I went down to investigate and recognised it as a German Motor Torpedo boat. These were high-speed craft, known as E-boats. The British equivalent was very similar, carrying two torpedoes, cannons, and machine guns, and had a crew of four. Propelled by two massive diesel engines, they gave the craft a top speed of over 30 miles per hour. A close-up investigation of this one greeted me with a hail of unwelcome fire from armament, and as usual, the tracer shells all seemed to be heading directly for me. I backed off and decided upon my method of attack. I waited for what seemed to be hours until I was sure I was well within range and opened up with all six guns. After a prolonged burst, I withdrew and surveyed the scene. The E-boat continued firing until I was out of range. I went in again and repeated the attack. Once again, I looked from a safe distance and then made another attack. The E-boat was silent, with no return fire, and it was motionless. Success. I reported its position in case Operations Control wanted to send out a naval party to take it in tow. I was given a confirmed "KILL" - one E-boat. Presumably, all the crew were dead, but I know not.

Later the same week, I was on readiness and, with my number two, was scrambled. A plane had been picked up by radar, approaching Bône and its harbour, and was at an altitude of upwards of ten thousand feet. I spotted him some distance off, and as we climbed up, he put the plane into a very steep dive and lined up for the harbour. We stood no chance of catching him, and he dropped a bomb. It was an Italian fighter bomber. He completed his dive and made off. We were well outside our range of fire. I heard later that his bomb scored a direct hit on the "Ajax" - a British naval craft which was well known later for its part in the Battle of the River Plate, together with the "Achilles" and "Exeter". This episode will be mentioned later in the book and concerns someone I met twenty-odd years later.

Units of the American First Army passed through on their way to the front line. Seeing them all wearing a medal was strange and a little pathetic. When questioned, we were told that it was the Algeria and

Tunisia Campaign Medal - and they hadn't even got to the fighting zone at the time. In fact, it appeared that they were issued the medal on their way across the Atlantic. How similar and yet how different are the Americans compared with the British? I understood that their rations included items such as tinned chicken, other mouth-watering delicacies, and occasionally, ice cream!

Sour grapes? I expect that there may be a bit of that lurking about.

Chapter 17

The Festive Season 1942

We were well into December; this would be my third Christmas in the RAF. I cannot remember anything about Christmas 1940 or Christmas 1941. They just came and went without being noticed. This one, however, was to be different, as you will read later in this chapter.

Tent life, of course, continued, and an aspect of it occasionally worried me. It seemed to me that we were very vulnerable each night as a tent, however sturdy, offered little protection against the objects the German Night Raiders aimed at us. We had antiaircraft guns in the vicinity, but I never saw or heard of any being shot down.

So, I hatched a plan to try to ensure a more peaceful night. I had noticed a white building on the coast near Bône. It was a hotel of some sort in more peaceful times, and it was remarkably like the one shown on the postcard marked "The Casino, Du Djelli".

a 1930s postcard of The Casino

Every time I flew over it, the building seemed empty. So I suggested to my friend that we take up residence there for a spell. I cannot remember exactly how we arrived each night, but we did. We chose a room, but there was no furniture of any description. We slept on the floor, and apart from the few times that a German plane on its way back to its base would give the place a squirt of machine gun fire, just for the hell of it - we had very peaceful nights. After a time, we were told to rejoin the lads in the tents, which, of course, we did. However, I suggested to the CO that it would not be a bad idea for all the pilots to move into the "Casino". The idea was not adopted, and so we returned to tent life.

As Christmas approached, we were all growing a bit tired of it all, and this feeling manifested in different ways. One evening, after flying had ceased, we were sitting or lying in our spaces in the tent. Of course, there was the usual conversation about the day's operations, card playing, etc., as happened every evening. But this particular night was different.

I had vaguely heard somewhere about Russian Roulette, but I suppose I didn't really know exactly what it meant. I was about to find out. A pilot from the London area decided he had had enough, really, and decided to test fate. All pilots carried a Smith and Wesson .38 revolver, which carried six shells. He flicked open the chamber and emptied all the shells, proclaiming at the same time what he was about to do.

Immediately, loud shouts arose to discourage him from going through with it. He was not deterred from his resolve. He loaded one shell, closed the chamber, and spun it around. In a flash, he put the muzzle against his temple and pulled the trigger. Everyone was stunned into silence and watched him in unbelievable amazement. The trigger clicked, but the gun did not fire. He smiled and looked all around. He quickly spun the chamber and did the same thing again. Nothing happened, so he refilled the chamber and returned the revolver to its holster. There was still a terrible silence as he looked around the tent, stood up, and said: "I shall come through this war alive!" He was wrong. Although this episode has taken a long time to describe, it was, in fact, over quite quickly, and although it was strange in a way that no one tried to stop him except by a few remarks such as: "Don't be a clot!" - and the like; he was a chap who was not really liked, hence the reluctance to interfere. He survived until the New Year when he, as they say, 'bought it!'

About this time, I had a very good number two. He was very new to the game, but he was keen to please and become proficient at flying Spitfires. He said at one time that he had never tried a flick roll. This is where you make the aircraft rapidly roll along its longitudinal axis. I told him, "For God's sake - don't try it!" A flick roll was the same manoeuvre as a slow or victory roll, but was, as the name implies, a vicious roll, and the machine just flicked its way into the roll, which was very fast. Once the Spitfire started flicking, it was highly unlikely that any pilot would recover stability. Like the "flat spin" I mentioned earlier, there is no answer to it. On my way back one day from an operation, he was wound up, as you might say, and decided to give it a try. It is very sad to relate that he just kept on flicking until he and his plane disintegrated on hitting the ground. What a shame and what a waste.

I called the Chapter "The Festive Season," and it was now fast approaching. I had heard stories about the soldiers in the First World War— the 1914/1918 slaughter—and how, on Christmas Eve or Christmas Day, the shelling and hand-to-hand fighting ceased for a period, and the opposing sides resting in their trenches heard the strains of "Silent Night" and other carols. All was peaceful—until the next day, when all hell broke loose again. As Christmas approached, I wondered if any such incident would happen to us, certainly not in the same manner, as we were some way behind the Army front line. I did think, though, that perhaps air operations would cease for a couple of days. Not a bit of it!

I was growing increasingly tired of it all, and the day before Christmas Eve, I found myself involved yet again. Although those last two words, "yet again," are rather stupid, as this was exactly what we were there for - an air battle in the region of Mejez El Bab. I was up against an ME-109 and got it in my sights. As I fired, a great lump fell off his port wing; as far as I was concerned, he was a goner. However, as neither I nor anyone else saw him bail out, I was granted a "PROBABLE" and not a "CONFIRMED." No doubt, hitting the target gives one a sense of gratification, but by that evening, it had worn off, and everything was back to routine.

By Christmas Eve, there would be no let-up, and we had our orders for Christmas Day. War was war, I suppose. I was beginning to get very tired and needed a break, but as we had lost quite a number of the squadron Pilots, there was no respite. I decided, therefore, that I must do something about it to try to relieve the tension.

For the first time in my life, I got hold of a bottle of wine. In hindsight, I suppose it was a bottle of cheap Algerian plonk, but nevertheless, I drank the whole bottle. This made me feel a little better, and I cursed myself for not having done the same thing many times before. The next morning came all too soon, and I got out of my sleeping bag. I don't have to tell you how I felt! My stomach and brain were still paralysed, and although I managed to dress, I did not leave the tent but sat near the paraffin stove and thought I was dying. One of the pilots came back and said, "The CO wants you to take off in five minutes." "Tell him I'm ill," I said. He came himself and recognised the symptoms. He ordered me to take off. I refused. "If you don't fly," he said, "I'll court-martial you." I answered that I was not capable of flying. "Court-martial it is then," he said.

That sort of disobedience in the "field" could mean being shot on the spot. I felt so ill that even the thought of that didn't worry me. The CO left me alone all that day, and as I turned up the next morning, I think he and I were both relieved. I heard nothing more about it. One or two drinks to relieve the tensions of the future months may well have been beneficial, but I never risked it. Foolish, I know, but there you are.

The Pioneer Corps or Royal Electrical and Mechanical Engineers (or whoever they were who had the bulldozers!) had prepared three landing strips covering a distance of about half to three-quarters of a mile in a fairly flat valley east of Mejez El Bab, and shortly after the New Year, we moved there. It was certainly a good idea to have three spaced-out strips, and they were called "Piccadilly", "Victoria", and "Leicester Square". So, at least three squadrons of Spitfires were now operating from the same region. I cannot remember the name of the Wing Commander.

Shortly after the move, two things happened. My old pal from Gourock Harbour and the "SS Stratheden" days was posted. I honestly don't know how it came about, but he ended up on a squadron in Burma somewhere. Strange happenings! The other thing was that I was posted, a matter of a few hundred yards to No. 232 Squadron, who had been hit very badly.

The front line was, to say the least, rather fluid, but overall, the

Armies were steadily gaining ground. It will perhaps be opportune to mention "The Bomb Line". Each squadron had a map of the area, which was kept by the CO. He would stick pins in specific locations, and a piece of string would join the pins. He would adjust the pins and lines as he received daily information about frontline movements. This was called "The Bomb Line," and all targets east of it were fair game. Our operations were not confined to high altitudes; we conducted a significant amount of work against ground targets, particularly in response to Army requests. I recall being tasked with attacking a German artillery post that was causing a great deal of trouble. I found it and went down. Four German soldiers operated the post, and after two or three attacks, I looked back and saw them all slumped over the sandbags or lying on the floor. Whose sons were they? I wondered.

But my most distasteful target was a field containing horses. As the Germans began to run short of fuel, they started using horses, which had been spotted. I just flew back and forth and killed or wounded as many as possible. This close cooperation system with the Army was used increasingly as the war continued. A pilot would be sent up to the front line, transmit from the ground, and give targets to some planes flying around for the very purpose. This was called a "Taxi Rank" and was very successful.

The new squadron was, of course, much the same as the last one, but I had another problem—life these days seemed to be full of problems. For some weeks, I had been bothered by a toothache, and this was getting worse—far worse.

I had a word with my new CO, who was quite sympathetic. "I have heard," he said, "a dentist has arrived or is about to arrive in Setif. Take your plane and get it seen to." So off I went and landed on the strip at Setif. I found the dentist in a house which the Army had requisitioned. It was at a crossroads just outside the village. In I went. He looked surprised to see me and said that he had only just arrived. In the room was a table and a chair. I told him the trouble, an incessant toothache. He looked at it and then pronounced his diagnosis. "It needs to come out," he said, "but all I have is a pair of forceps. All my equipment is on its way somewhere". He could not say when it would arrive. "I'll take it out for you," he said, "if you are desperate?" I thought for a few seconds and decided that it was now or never. The CO wouldn't let me keep coming back here. "Yes," I said, "take it out, but disregard my scream!" "All you will feel," he said, "is my pushing down very hard on your jaw. Then there will be a second of jarring pain, and it will be all over." I sat down in the chair, sweating with fear. It was exactly as he said.

I suppose the whole thing took about five seconds. He didn't mess about, for which I was grateful. He inspected the hole in the gum. "Fine," he said, "take these aspirins with you and use them as you think fit." As you can imagine, I thanked him and walked out of the place feeling very light-hearted. I was glad it was all over, but I hoped it would never happen again. The Festive Season was now well past, as we were already in February.

Chapter 18

The Campaign Continues

February brought a lovely surprise in the way of three or four days' leave. I was very grateful to get away from the squadron for a break. As I recall, I somehow arrived at Constantine, where a building had been requisitioned and converted into a sort of rest centre. I took things very easily indeed and spent a fair time wandering around the streets and narrow ways between the houses. It was strange to see the Arab men squatting outside their homes, entirely covered by their long white gowns. They would stare at you, which was understandable, and one occasionally felt a sense of fear. I put a great deal of faith in the "Goolie Chit", which we all carried at all times. Let me explain. This was a slang name for a card with a message printed in three or four languages, including a couple of Arabic dialects. The message said that a substantial reward would be given if the Bearer was returned safely and unharmed to the British or Allied Forces. It was said that certain Arab tribes delighted in removing the testicles from strangers - hence a chit to save the goolies or testicles.

I was walking one morning when two very excited children approached me. A boy of about six and his sister of about nine years old. They were French-speaking, and I gathered from their excited speech and gestures that their parents would like me to join them for lunch at their house. Well - that was different, wasn't it?

We arrived at an apartment block and went up to the first floor. The children were very excited, as though they had just caught a big fish, and showed me the way into a large dining room. Father and Mother greeted me sincerely and offered me a drink of wine. I took it, but it lasted me all the way through lunch. They were very polite, and a young couple joined us at the table. The young lady had a very young baby. Lunch began with a soup that was very nice indeed. A meat course and side salad followed this. I immediately felt at home and decided I could not sit down to eat while wearing a revolver. I, therefore, removed the belt and hung the gun and belt on a hook on the wall. Stupid? You may think so, but it worked out very well. I managed to converse a little, and it was a pleasant affair. Much to my amazement, halfway through the meal, the baby started crying, and without further ado and without the slightest embarrassment, she unbuttoned her dress and proceeded to feed the baby as though it was the natural thing to do. Well, of course it was. I suppose that it is the British who have weird ideas about these things.

I was very grateful for having had a good foundation in French and for continuing to learn the subject after leaving school. Nevertheless, I had to ask them to speak slowly continually, and we just about got by. As I departed, they insisted that I return in the future, but of course, I never saw Constantine again.

When I returned to the squadron, I felt somewhat refreshed, but I was immediately back into the same old business. Strange to say, but we experienced heavy night showers. These were welcomed to collect water that was sometimes in short supply. February passed, and we entered March, when a very surprising thing happened at the beginning of the month.

The CO took me aside and said, "Congratulations, Flying Officer, you have been commissioned." I looked at the CO and was speechless. "Will you say that again?" I said. "Your commission has come through," he said, "and because it is back-dated to the 1st August 1942, you are now a Flying Officer". The rule was that if you survive six months as a Pilot Officer, you are automatically promoted one rank up. I could not believe it. The interview for the commission, which took place back in July 1942, had long since been lost in the mists of time, as they say. I was always under the impression that I had failed the interview because I had not answered a couple of questions on the form that I considered irrelevant. But apparently not, I had sailed through. What a pity I had been sent on my travels before the news reached me. It was now seven months since the commission had been granted. It was a good job I was still alive to receive the news!

Armed with a razor blade, I unpicked the Sergeant's stripes from my uniform, unpinned the brass crown above them and scrounged a couple of Flying Officer epaulette braids, and that, for the time being, was all I needed. The first benefit was a move to a two-person tent with a decent camp bed. Although we were in North Africa and on the coastal strips, we were not all that far from the desert, and the nights were cold indeed. As was (and still is) my want, I had amassed thirteen blankets - eight underneath and five on top - or was it the other way around? Anyway, I was as snug as a bug in a rug, as they say. So much so that I pulled the blankets back one morning to get out of bed, only to find that I had been sleeping all night with a scorpion between my legs. He was quite friendly, however, and must have also spent a warm and comfortable night. During the rainy nights, I fitted sheep's horns to my camp bed legs - this successfully kept my bottom out of the water, which used to pervade the tent during these storms.

I was still rather amazed by the commission business. I had written it off long ago, but it was very pleasing to be promoted. There was also a certain amount of pleasure in coming up through the ranks, as they say. That may sound rather stupid and parochial, but there you are.

Commissioned or non-commissioned, the pilots were much the same. Unlike the other Military Services, the RAF was the first (if not the only) service to amalgamate the two Messes and call it an Aircrew Mess. This came, I believe, late in the war, but it was a very sensible move.

We saw little of the Army, except from the air, when we operated near them. The Spitfire was a truly exceptional fighting machine that could be utilised in a wide range of roles. At that time in the war, there was no real air-to-ground attack plane. The Typhoon was just about to come into service, but certainly not in our sphere.

Around this time in 1943, the Americans arrived with their medium bombers, such as the Boston and Marauder, which were stationed somewhere near Algiers. Unfortunately for us, their bomb lines must have been out of date for some time, as on two occasions, our landing strips and encampments were the recipients of some American bombs. It served me right, I suppose, for having had a go at an American Tomahawk fighter back at the beginning of 1942! The CO did remark, however, that if they came again, we would shoot the buggers down! That would have caused a stir, wouldn't it? The transatlantic phone lines would have been red hot.

I must mention here a bit of trade I conducted with the Americans. As previously discussed, the Americans were very well-fed indeed and had lots of chocolate bars and cigarettes, but the one thing they did not have was booze. Strangely, we did - I think the ration was supposed to be one bottle of whisky per month, and we got a certain number of circular air-tight tins of cigarettes. Someone laid down the rations somewhere, but of course, what one got was a different matter. However, I did manage to amass a stock of five bottles of whisky by fair means or foul. The point is that I swapped my whisky stock for an American Jeep. Can you imagine! Where I was going to go in it and what I was going to do with it, I could not imagine.

Nevertheless, I used to bash around in it locally, and I lent it to others who promised to be very careful drivers. It was great fun! When we eventually moved on to an airfield between Tunis and Bizerta on the northern point of Tunisia, I gave it to my fitter and never saw the jeep again. Easy come, easy go, as they say.

Back to the more serious business of flying. There was always the possibility of having to force land over enemy territory - or Bedouin Arab territory, for that matter. I mentioned the Goolie chit, but we always carried an escape pack. This was a neat pack containing high-food-value chocolate, a small compass, a file shrouded in soft rubber, and maps of the area printed on silk. As well as their obvious uses as aids to returning to base, these items, it was said, were designed so that, in extremes, they could be secreted in one or more hiding places in the body.

To supplement these items, I added one of my own. I always had a pack of 200 cigarettes strapped to the aircraft radio, which was housed in a compartment to the rear of the cockpit. These cigarettes did, in fact, become very useful—but more of that later.

Chapter 19

The Final Stages of "Torch"

Cooperation with the Army was good, effective, and improving. At least that was my view, but certainly not one I held alone. I mention this as a preamble to two more off-beat incidents. I was on one occasion up in the Army lines for a day, but as it happened, on this occasion, there was no communicating and directing my section of the squadron on what to do. This enabled me to try out an artillery piece. I suppose you would call it a small field gun that fired twelve-pound shells. I had a quick lesson in range finding and aiming, and fired my shell aimed at a small building some distance away. I was delighted when I hit the target. It was different from pressing the gun button in the cockpit of an aeroplane. The next piece of equipment I was privileged to try was a flamethrower. This had a backpack and was handheld. What a weapon — I immediately thought of the poor recipient! I was glad to relieve myself of it. "Everyman to his trade," I said. I suppose this personal type of Army cooperation was counted as a day off. It must have been because days off seemed nonexistent. Not that there was anywhere to go except one's tent!

I do not recall moving forward from our landing site and continued to conduct all our operations from Mejez El Bab. A German Fighter Wing stationed nearby in Bizerta was giving us a lot of trouble. They were Focke-Wulf 190s, and we were continually having a go at each other. That sounds rather jolly and like a game of rugby or something, but unfortunately, it was serious stuff.

During one of these confrontations, I was credited with a confirmed "KILL", which somewhat boosted my ego. I suppose it helped the campaign in a tin-pot way, although it added to my pathetic score. It seemed to me—and probably to others too—that I didn't have the knack for this air-to-air combat; although I could fly a fighter very well indeed, perhaps my efforts would have been more effective in some other facet of the trade. It might at this juncture be opportune to list the rules of a fighter pilot, but I must say that I did not come across these rules until many years later, although I had learned them by experience rather than formal education.

This document was headed "Ten Rules For Air Fighters" - but was commonly called "The Ten Commandments":

- Wait until you see "the whites of their eyes"—fire short bursts of one to two seconds, and only when your sights are definitely on.
- While shooting, think of nothing else. Brace the whole body. Concentrate on your ring sight.
- Always keep a sharp lookout. "Keep your finger out!"
- Height gives you the initiative.
- Always turn and face the attack.
- Make your decision promptly. It is better to act quickly, even though your tactics are not the best.
- Never fly straight and level in a combat zone for over thirty seconds.
- When diving to attack, always leave a proportion of your formation above to act as top guard.
- Initiative, aggression, air discipline, and teamwork are words that mean something in air fighting.
- Go in quickly, punch hard, get out.

I should think that rule number one was probably a leftover from the 1914–18 war, when aircraft speeds were so low that it would have been possible to lean out of the cockpit and shake hands with your opponent.

However, they are good rules. As I said, it was a pity to have learned them by experience rather than tuition. I certainly had the luck to survive, although what I lacked was an aggressive nature, and this is essential.

However, back to the campaign, I have two or three more events to relate. Firstly, I refer back to the pack of two hundred cigarettes strapped to the radio. Around this time, we were once again engaged in a melee when I was hit with quite a thump. I do not know whether it was a cannon shell from a German fighter or an anti-aircraft shell from the ground. We were operating at a much lower level than usual, so it may have been either, but what is certain is that I never saw it coming—and those are the ones that get you. The offending shell (or shells) hit me just behind the cockpit and blew a large hole right through to the other side of the aircraft and took my radio - and my cigarettes! - out into space. Although the aircraft was still flyable, it was rather bumpy, and I disengaged myself from the scrap and returned to base.

I landed safely, feeling glad to be in one piece, but at the same time, I felt rather disgusted. The aircraft was set aside to be repaired when possible, and I took over another machine. I was not sorry about losing that particular Spitfire, as I had complained on more than one occasion to the fitter that at around 20 thousand feet, the engine was prone to coughing and spluttering and momentarily lost power. The fitter had done all he could to check carburation and other aspects, but the occasional fault persisted and was unnerving. I sometimes thought the fitter had begun to disbelieve me, but it was the truth. I was not sorry to see that machine go.

All of this leads me to relate that around this time, I had a number two, a "newish" pilot who hailed from the Birmingham area. It very soon became evident that this lad was always making excuses of various sorts to avoid the obvious dangers of operations—excuses such as sickness, malfunctions of his plane, headaches, poor sight or any old thing. Consequently, when the action started, he was missing. After having spoken with him on several occasions, I gave him a final warning about his behaviour. We were all in the same boat, and having someone continually opt out was, to say the least, undesirable. In the end, I reported him to the CO, and shortly afterwards, he disappeared. I gathered he was posted as LMF* and returned to the UK. I neither knew nor cared what happened to him, but I presume he would be sent to Eastchurch, where all those of a similar nature were sent, and would likely find other employment. It is not a very nice thing to happen, but at the same time, this sort of cowardice, for whatever reason, could not really be tolerated.

The campaign progressed day by day, and it became fairly obvious that we were on the winning side, although it was far from a capitulation. There was always that slight fear that there would be a reversal of fortunes. At the end of April or early May 1943, an amazing thing happened. Amazing, because I have never heard of the occurrence before, or, for that matter, since. I do not mean to say that it never happened to anyone else; I only say that I have never heard of it.

Just west of Tunis, at our normal operating height of around 20 thousand feet, we were engaged in a battle, and at one point, I really was in trouble! To avoid being blown out of the sky, I shoved the propeller pitch fully forward, along with the throttle, which I rammed "through the gate". This gave absolute maximum power, and it served its purpose. According to the book, this maximum power use was limited; otherwise, the engine would "blow up". This took but a few minutes, and I was fully conscious of it. At the same time, using this absolute boost meant the fuel was devoured at an alarming rate. It was rather like opening a bath tap. I expect you now know the outcome. Yes - I ran out of fuel. You can imagine the resulting concern, to put it mildly.

I emerged from the battle and quickly decided upon my action plan. I could bail out, but the result would be parachuting into enemy territory. No, I thought, I will choose the optimum rate of descent and head westwards over the range of mountains and see how it goes. It went very well indeed, and I just quietly proceeded towards the base, hoping that I still had sufficient height to reach it.

There are strict rules about crash landings: they must always be performed with the wheels up, thus landing and sliding along on the belly of the aircraft, not on the landing strip (or runway) but alongside it. I could, of course, should I reach the vicinity of the landing strip, head

---

* LMF stands for Lack of Moral Fibre. It was a term used by the British Royal Air Force (RAF) to describe aircrew who refused to fly operations, often due to psychological trauma, fear, or mental breakdowns under the extreme pressures of aerial combat.

the aircraft away from it, and jump out. I considered all these options, and, given the success of things up to now, I decided to try the ultimate. I selected "wheels down" as I had no engine and, consequently, no hydraulic power. I shook the aircraft as violently as I could from side to side and waited to hear the "clunk" of the legs being locked in the down position. The green lights came on for both wheels. I felt quite elated. What if I could get my height and approach just right for the end of the landing strip and shove the thing down without a scrap of damage! I was committed now and did my "S" bends to get myself in the correct position to land. It worked, and I managed a superb landing. The Spitfire brakes are worked by air and not by hydraulics. It came to a halt, and I jumped out. I was walking on air, not a blemish! I said to myself: "That's a damn good bit of flying", and walked to report to the CO.

I told him what had happened. "Go and get your Log Book," he said, which I did whilst thinking of the commendation he would write in it in green ink. He wrote in it and gave it back to me. I opened it and got the shock of my life. The writing was in red ink, not green. The endorsement stated horrible words, such as defiance of the rules, etc. I was disgusted and said that the aeroplane was out there unscathed. He said, "Never mind the Spitfire—I could have lost a pilot." So there you are. You never know, do you? I suppose you should obey the rules!

Things didn't seem to be going very well in other directions. I received a letter from the Officers Pay section of the Air Ministry, which informed me that they had opened a bank account in my name in Lloyds Bank in London, and they had credited me with my Officer's pay backdated to the first of August 1942 - that amount of my pay should have been as a Flight Sergeant. Strange to say, there is very little difference between the pay of a Flight Sergeant and a Pilot Officer. This was a blow. It would have been correct and vastly different if they had said that they had deducted the Flight Sergeant's pay I had drawn. There was really no reason to draw much pay, and I had not done so. I explained this dilemma to the CO, who said he would do his best, but circumstances prevented me from pursuing the matter further. Consequently, I lost what was to me a lot of money. I also lost a significant amount of pay later on, which will be described at the appropriate time in the memoirs. Financially, I wasn't doing too well in this war, but at least I was still alive.

By mid-May, optimism about the end of the campaign had increased. The Eighth Army and its colleagues in the east of Tunisia, and the Allied Armies in our sphere, were doing a magnificent job, and the end was all but in sight.

I was getting exhausted. I had completed the requisite number of operational flying hours for the tour and was well into the second tour. I considered, therefore, that I was due for the prescribed rest. I decided that I must do something about it. I cannot remember the exact date, but the news was that we had finally won the North African campaign, and the Germans and their Italian allies had been driven out of North Africa. It was obvious that the next stage would be the invasion of mainland Europe.

However, we flew up to an airfield between Tunis and Bizerta. There were very few of the original pilots left. By that, I mean the ones who had seen the whole campaign through. We landed at our new temporary base and spent a short time on sorties, ensuring that all pockets of resistance had been overcome. At that time, I heard of an area nearby that was full of enemy vehicles of all kinds. So off I went to investigate. To cut a long story short, I became the owner of a Citroën coupe, which was all alone amongst this lot with the keys in it, just as it had been dumped. We were told we were to have a sort of holiday and spend a few days with our tents on the beach near Carthage. This was wonderful, and I toured extensively in my Citroën. The Ground Crew saw our aircraft, and then they were all shipped to Malta. So that was our next destination!

One evening, the CO received a message instructing us to return to our aircraft, to take off shortly after dawn, and fly at zero feet to Malta. We went to the airfield, and I said farewell to my motor car and wondered what its future would be. Around dawn, we boarded our aircraft and started them up, went through the usual checks, and took off. This was it - I thought. I will get some rest when I get to Malta, and I look forward to it.

There was an occasion, before setting off to Malta, when we were all told to smarten ourselves up (quite how that could be accomplished, I don't know) and assemble for a parade to be greeted and congratulated by our leader, the renowned Winston Churchill. We all stood there in the very hot sun for a long time, but he never showed up, so we dispersed in an angry mood. We were all very happy about the victory and were slightly dismayed when Winston announced via some medium or other:

"This victory was not the beginning of the end, but merely the end of the beginning".

Not a very generous remark!

Chapter 20

A Change is as Good as a Rest

It has often been said, "that a change is as good as a rest". Is it? Well, we shall see.

We crossed the coast, and I saw that the Commanding Officer had chosen a course that was all but due east. It was going to be another beautiful day. Since this flight was at a very low level (to avoid German radar operating from Sicily), it was unlikely that we would encounter any opposition. I was looking forward to a peaceful flight for a change. Quite suddenly, I saw a small puff of white exhaust smoke come from one of the exhaust stubs. Surely not, I thought. I knew precisely what white smoke indicated; it meant the mechanical failure of the engine, and I waited with very bated breath for another sign. There was nothing for a minute or two, and then, to my horror, another puff and another, and eventually a steady stream. I looked at the radiator temperature gauge; it was climbing.

I opened the radiator flap to allow more cold air to circulate. This had no effect whatsoever. This was indeed trouble, and we were over the sea to add to the bargain. I switched to transmit: "Blue One" (or whatever my colour was at that time) "Blue One to Leader - Glycol Leak - Switching off." I had two options: ditch it in the sea or try to climb to a sufficient height, then bail out. The engine was still running, and although the ride was bumpy, it maintained flying speed. I decided to get some height, if possible. I didn't fancy ditching as a Spitfire would sink seven seconds after coming to rest on the sea. I immediately pulled the knob and jettisoned the hood, then pulled the radio plug out and removed my helmet, throwing it out. I was no longer in touch with the other aircraft.

Gently, I climbed, maintaining an easterly course. I managed around two thousand feet in fits and starts before the engine seized up, and the propeller came to rest. I knew all the procedures off by heart for the various escape methods. Turn the plane on its back and try to kick the stick forward as you get out. This helps to eject you from the cockpit. The dinghy is located between your bottom and the parachute, and just before you hit the sea, the parachute harness should be released. This automatically pulls the cover off the dinghy, and theoretically, it should land in the sea near you. There is a small bottle of compressed gas attached to the dinghy. You turn it on, and the dinghy inflates.

I started the routine, and as I turned the aircraft onto its back, I saw two little pimples of land protruding through a morning mist. I kept turning, brought the plane upright again, and inspected the new find. Yes - it was land of some sort, but what and where? Maps of the area were practically non-existent, and in any case, I certainly didn't have one. Anyway, I thought it was better to land one way or the other near land than in the middle of the sea. I put my straps back on and decided to take a look, hoping to crash the thing onto terra firma. This was a third option that, just a short time before, had not been considered at all. As I circled down, the rest of the squadron also circled once or twice, and when they saw what I was about to do, they turned east and went on their way. As I descended, I reached a height too low for parachuting, so I was now really committed.

Eventually, I saw that the land was, in fact, a tiny island with a couple of extinct volcanoes rising from it. I searched for a flat spot to land. The best and really the only place was a stretch on the east side of the island, so I made my preparations. I did some "S" bends to get my approach and height correct for the crash landing. I tightened the straps and pulled them repeatedly. On the final approach, I turned off the petrol and all switches and lowered the seat fully. I was approaching too fast, so I pulled back on the stick once or twice, but it didn't seem to make much difference. I was quickly running out of time, and as you will realise, a second attempt was impossible. In a few seconds, I mentally reviewed the procedure for a belly landing, and I had covered everything that needed to be done. Just before I touched down, I glanced at the airspeed indicator and realised I was travelling far too fast, but I could do nothing about it.

There was a loud crunch, and bits of the propeller flew off. I hit what seemed to be a sort of stone wall. Many years later, when I returned to the island and saw that there were no stone walls in that area, I knew I must have ploughed through a wall of cactus plants about three or four feet high. Nevertheless, the result was that it threw me into a cartwheel. This violent motion dislodged both wings, and I barreled on. After a few more obstacles, I somersaulted twice and lost the back half of the fuselage. I was conscious of all this happening, and finally, what was left of the Spitfire turned over and screwed its nose into a mound. At long last, I was motionless. There was no sound, no feeling, no sight. I literally thought I was dead.

I do not know how long I remained in this position, but gradually, the phosphorescent instruments began to come into view. My head was pounding, but I thought - at least I could see. Sometime later, I realised that my shoulders bore all the weight of my body. I was upside down. So I could see, and I could feel, and yet all was in darkness, and all was quiet. The plane is upside down, and I have ploughed into the ground was the final realisation.

On the small door on the left-hand side of the cockpit of a Spitfire, two clips hold a metal claw bar. I felt for it and started trying to cut the door open. Eventually, I was successful and managed to dig my way out. I stood up and tried my limbs - everything seemed to work. I surveyed the scene. I could see the sea in the distance. "Right," I said to myself, "I'll get the dingy and my small kit" (not forgetting the two hundred cigarettes which I had replaced). I pulled the cover off the dinghy, got my bits and pieces, and set off for the beach. I didn't know where on earth I was, but the squadron knew, and I would set sail for Malta. The chances were that there would be a westerly breeze, and it should blow me there. I should be spotted on the way.

I now realised that I was covered in blood and something was wrong with an eyelid. However, I set off. I had not gone very far when soldiers with pointed rifles stood up from behind cactus bushes. I dropped the things I was carrying, removed the revolver lanyard from around my neck, unbuckled the gun belt, and threw it on the ground. The soldiers advanced, and I passed out and sank to the ground.

I awoke sometime later, but I have absolutely no idea how long it was; however, upon awakening, I felt extremely uncomfortable. I was being jolted, and every part of my body seemed to be extremely painful. I was on an ass or mule and was being supported by an Italian soldier on each side. I felt absolutely terrible and paid no heed to the party of men who surrounded me. Both knees were bandaged and appeared enormous, as, in fact, they were. I had a headbandage covering my forehead and my left eye. They certainly had performed some excellent first aid. The journey, which I suppose was about a mile or less, seemed to be endless. Eventually, the track finished, and we arrived at a village. I was carried into the front room of a house, where they laid me on a bed, removed my shirt, shorts, shoes, and socks, and put me to bed. One soldier remained in the bedroom, sitting in a chair and gazing at me. I noticed that my clothing and small kit for washing had been placed on a table, together with - believe it or not - my two hundred cigarettes.

I dozed off into sleep and was glad of it. If you were to ask me how long it had been since the first puff of white exhaust smoke, I could not tell you. It was an absolute lifetime, and so much had happened in a comparatively short space of time. I don't know how many times I awoke to see the soldier still sitting there, and then fell asleep again. I was very sore and ached all over, but the rest was bliss. This wasn't quite the rest period I had wanted, but it was certainly a change!

Later on, I awoke to find a chap bending over me and offering me a drink. It was coffee, strong and sweet, and was most acceptable. He spoke to me in Italian, which I did not understand. I tried English, which he did not understand. I said that I could speak some French. He understood, and so we had some common ground. He told me he was a doctor from the Italian Navy and was the doctor for the island, and it was he who administered first aid at the crash site. He removed the bandages from my knees and examined them, and although they were extremely swollen, at least they both worked, and I had no broken bones. It was a miracle. He gave me an injection in my behind, I suppose to counter any infection. Then he thoroughly examined the rest of my body and kept saying "bene bene" (good, good). He then carefully removed the bandages from my head. He examined the gash on my forehead and then the upper lid of my left eye. He seemed quite satisfied and left the room, returning immediately with a mirror, which he held up for me to see my face. I could not believe what I saw; it was terrible. Bloody, bruised, and an eyelid hanging down in the middle. It was fortunate indeed that the eyelid was still connected at both ends. How it had been sliced - I presume by flying splinters - without damaging the eye, is unbelievable. The doctor made signs and said a few words. I understood that he was taking me to his surgery to stitch up the wounds.

A couple of soldiers came in bearing a stretcher, and they deposited me onto it. Off we went to a building on the only main street. It turned out to be the Police Station. I was laid on a table, and the doctor gave me another injection. He stitched the gash on the forehead first, then turned his attention to the eyelid. He was highly efficient and caring, and when he had finished, he surveyed his handiwork—a plaster and a bandage — and I was done. I thanked him. Perhaps he was only too glad to practise his art, but in the days to follow, we became pretty good friends.

Before I left the surgery to be carried back to the house, Il Commandante came in. He was an Italian Army Captain who was in charge of the island. He asked some questions via the doctor's French, but I explained that as a Prisoner of War (POW), I was entitled to give only my Name, Rank, and Number, which I repeated several times. He seemed to be far more nervous than I was. I was beginning to settle down now, and it appeared that my landing on the island was the first thing that had happened to them since the war started. Everyone seemed to be very friendly, and I was treated more like a guest than an enemy.

Back to the bedroom. Drinks and meals came regularly, and I started walking around the bedroom as soon as possible. My shorts, shirt, and socks reappeared - all washed, and my Mae West had been cleaned up as much as possible. This was service indeed! The doctor visited me twice or three times daily to check that all was well and that I was on the road to recovery and regaining my health and mobility.

MAKE IT DO

Now that I was feeling more human, I spent as much time as I could walking around the room under the watchful eye of my guardian. The soldiers were obviously on round-the-clock shifts, and all seemed pleased, with an understandable curiosity about this British man who had descended upon them. I had plenty of time to think. I thought of my position, what I could do, and my future. I quickly learned the first dreadful lesson about being a Prisoner of War. It was simply that one did not know what the next move would be. And it was an ever-present worry. Where would I go? Would they dispose of me? What would happen? All these thoughts ran round and round in my head, and the result was that I ended up with an intolerable conclusion. You were entirely in the power of those in charge of you, and there was little you could do. Alright, you could kick up a fuss and shout and bawl, but in the end, it would make no difference. And yet, there I was. I had been treated with the utmost kindness and consideration, and I could not have received better medical attention.

The tiny speck of land that is Linosa

The island from above

The Island of Linosa was the smallest inhabited island of the Pelagic Group, and it lay about halfway between Tunis and Malta and about eighty miles south of Sicily. Apart from a couple of tiny islands, which were hardly more than volcanic rocks sticking out of the sea, Lampedusa was the only other island of any size. Linosa was approximately five miles long and about a mile wide at its widest point. If that! It was obvious that these two islands (but at the time, I knew not of Lampedusa) would be taken over by the Allies - probably the British - shortly after the invasion of Sicily, which was imminent. Having considered this, the next time the doctor visited with the Comandante, I mentioned it - via the doctor's French, of course - and that if they kept me here for a couple of weeks or so, I would ensure that they were also well treated after their capture. This seemed to meet with the Captain's approval, and he departed.

The doctor spoke with the guard and took me outside to assess my progress with walking. He was very pleased – and so was I. Once again, we returned to the bedroom, and he removed plaster and bandages to inspect the wounds. He was pleased and departed, saying he would return the next day to take me on a visit! What sort of a visit, I wondered. But the Captain came with him bearing a pencil and paper and asked if I would write down to the effect that I had been treated well. He could then hand this note to an invading force. I agreed, and without a second thought, wrote a verse about "Mary Had a Little Lamb." He departed like a dog with two tails.

The Doctor and I set off on our walk and eventually arrived at a cave in a hillside. This was 1943, and I could not believe my eyes when I saw some families still living in caves. We were welcomed by the housewife (or cave wife), and whilst she chatted with the doctor, she produced a cup of coffee each. Again, nothing but first-class hospitality. The cave seemed to be quite comfortable, and I was surprised. After half an hour, we gave our thanks and departed. During this little jaunt, I was astonished to notice that we did not have a guard with us. Perhaps, after all, I could stay on the island until the British arrived. It could be far worse - it was June and very warm, and I was not short of food. Shortly after our return to the little house where my room was, we were joined by the Captain yet again. He spoke a few words to the doctor, who then turned to me to relay the message. It was those renowned words: "For you, the war is over," or as it was said to me: "Pour vous, la guerre, c'est fini".

I don't know where the sentence originated, but it was well-known. It sounded very ominous and was backed by a whole world of meaning. There was a ring of finality about it, too - and yet life was not too bad. Then there was the underlying horror. I was completely in their power, and the uncertainty of the future always remained.

The Captain was furious! He had found a soldier in his troop who could read English! Mary and her lamb no longer fooled him, and he was mad. I could see that he was astounded that I should do such a thing after the way I had been looked after. Yes, he had a point, I suppose, so I wrote a note to the effect that since being a prisoner on this island from

5th June 1943, I had been treated exceptionally well, and that I requested that the Captain and his troops should be treated in the same manner. He went off, no doubt, to find his English-reading soldier. I heard no more about it. After a week or so, the doctor removed my stitches and made a final examination. Everything was fine, and I felt fine too, at least physically.

Chapter 21

The Boat Trip

After about ten days on Linosa, the Captain and the Doctor appeared in my room, it was late at night—how late—I do not know. This was June in the Mediterranean, and the days were long and bright. They woke me up, and I was told that they had received a signal from Rome saying I was to be moved off Linosa. So, they *had* reported my arrival in Linosa. I had hoped that this would not happen.

I dressed, put on my Mae West, picked up my small kit, cigarettes, and lighter, and placed them into my small holdall. We set off and walked through the village to the end of the main street. I had never been so far before, and we ended up at a small harbour. Standing by was a small motorised fishing boat. I boarded with two guards. I said farewell to Il Commandante and a sincere farewell to my friend, the Doctor. I was extremely grateful to him for his treatment of me, both medically and psychologically, especially because I was the enemy. I suppose his duties as a doctor superseded all other conditions. I offered him a somewhat meagre gift of two packets of cigarettes. He accepted these with evident sincerity, and I stepped aboard the boat, which set sail immediately.

Having now lost my French-speaking doctor friend, I was immediately plunged back into my own little world and listened to the two guards and two crew chattering away in a strange dialect of Italian. I was immediately tormented by the questions that had dominated my thoughts since the crash landing and were to be in my mind for a long time to come. Where am I going now? What is going to happen to me? What will my new captors be like? How shall I be treated? Shall I be alive in a week, or a day for that matter? I knew I must not become despondent; I had to endeavour to always look on the bright side, and I had to, at all times, remind them that I was a British officer. I shouldn't become belligerent, or I may well come off worst. The Continentals are much more rank-conscious than the British, so I kept that in mind. As we chugged along through the night, my thoughts returned to Linosa. I had been incredibly fortunate, firstly, to survive the crash and, secondly, to have been treated so very well.

Linosa had, at that time, about 200 inhabitants and was used during the 1939-45 war as a sort of prison island for the bad lads of the Italian services. It continued in this role after the war, and members of the Mafia were sent there. The islanders were impoverished and relied primarily on fishing. A few cattle survived on cacti. Some families, as I have explained, were living in caves. I do not doubt that mainland Italy provided more amenities for the Islanders as time passed. It would appear that my landing on the island was just about the only thing that happened to them during the war.

It probably took them very much by surprise, which no doubt was in my favour. Flying continuously over enemy territory is a hazardous endeavour, and although being taken prisoner is always a possibility, one does not think about it or prepare for it. I knew little of my rights as a Prisoner of War as specified in the Geneva Convention articles. Therefore, I had no option but to formulate my own form of behaviour and trust very much in luck; so far, my luck had held. Sometime in the autumn of 1945, I met a Wing Commander who, during my interview with him to decide on my future, discovered that he knew my story about Linosa. It was he, while stationed in Malta, who had alerted the Marines dispatched from Malta to Linosa. The purpose of this landing party was to get me off the island. A section of Spitfires was sent to view the island at close range. They saw what remained of my aeroplane and, after giving the village a few bursts of gunfire, turned back and reported that it would have been impossible to survive such a crash landing. That naval craft, with its little invasion force of

Marines, was turned back! "That's life," as they say. But now, back to the story.

The little fishing boat chugged through the darkness, and all on board seemed oblivious to my presence. They were quite correct in their assumption that I was not about to jump overboard, and all continued their conversations. I knew it was my bounded duty to escape - but I had to be sensible about it. Perhaps a better opportunity would present itself at a later date. Once again, I began to feel rather lonely. Where were we going? What was in store?

After a couple of hours or more, we arrived in what appeared to be a much larger harbour, and the two guards came closer to me. Very soon, we three climbed out, and a lorry was waiting, which we immediately climbed into. A very short journey brought us to a doorway on the side of a small hill. On being shepherded through the door, I found myself in a large cave with beds arranged in a circle. It was a hospital of sorts, and I was shown to a bed, where they motioned for me to lie down on it. The guards left me, and I was then visited by a medic who gave me the once-over and left me. I tried to sleep. Morning came, and I was brought a mug of coffee and a piece of dry bread. This was prison indeed. I quickly learned that Italian hospitals do not provide food, and the other inmates were soon visited by their relatives or friends, who brought them breakfast. Some of the other patients were mobile; occasionally, they would come by my bed and talk to me. I tried my best to understand what they were saying, but with little success. For the next couple of days, I existed on watery soup with bits of pasta and dry bread. The fellow in the next bed was prone most of the time, but it was very noticeable that every time his wife appeared with his meal, he would put on an act of pain and misery, and this moaning and groaning continued during the whole of her visit. She was obviously tired of his pretence - although I do not doubt that he was suffering somewhat. I learned later that he had been the recipient of a shell from, believe it or not, a Spitfire attack! I can imagine his anger when he found out that the chap in the next bed was, in fact, a Spitfire pilot. Had he been mobile, I am sure he would have done me in! This antagonism, however, was not shared by his wife, who started to give me some of his food. Her motherly instinct had prevailed over all the circumstances, and I was extremely grateful.

It was, I think, the second night I was there, that there was a great commotion and sounds outside of gunfire and bombing. This went on most of the night. "It's an invasion," I thought - perhaps I shall soon be out of here and back with my fellow countrymen. It was obvious that the Allies would soon take control of this island and Linosa, as well as whatever else was in the vicinity. However, it was not to be—yet. It had been a sort of trial run to spy out the land. This was unfortunate indeed.

The toilet arrangements for the bedridden were the usual bedpans, and for the others, including myself, there was a one-seater toilet outside the cave. I learned that the Italian word was "cabinetto" - consequently, upon speaking this word, a guard appeared and conducted me to the little hut outside. The door was to be left open, and he stood facing me while the operation continued.

The morning after the raid, I had a visitor in the form of an English-speaking Army officer. How nice it was to hear my own language again after what seemed to be an age. Life is full of surprises, even in those untoward circumstances, and this officer informed me that during the raid the previous night, two British soldiers had been killed, and there was to be a funeral. "Would I like to attend?" he asked. "Of course I would," I said, donning my merge clothing. We walked a short distance to the cemetery, and I witnessed the service and burial. I memorised the two names and numbers for future use, but sadly, I eventually forgot them. On the way back, I asked the officer if he could find me some toothpaste, and he said he would try. Later that day, he appeared with the toothpaste at my bedside and stayed for a little chat. I don't remember what we talked about, but before he left, I gave him, in exchange, a picture postcard of the pin-up of the day - Dorothy Lamour! This seemed to please him, and off he went. I never saw him again. Please don't ask me how I came to have this picture in my possession, but it did come in handy anyway.

Life thereafter in this hospital consisted of endeavouring to read Italian in the occasional newspaper or magazine, thanking the good lady for her food presents, and making the occasional trip to the cabinetto. I do not recall how many days I spent there - I suppose it was just short of a week. Then, one night (why do they always do these things at night when it is impossible to see anything?), they put me into a truck for the return journey to the harbour. We arrived at the quayside and disembarked from the truck. Good heavens! What on earth was that alongside? It was a submarine!

I was very quickly escorted aboard, and the thing immediately set sail. I was taken below to what turned out to be the Officers' Mess, which consisted of four bunks, a table, and four chairs. The ship rumbled off into the night.

It turned out that I had missed the invasion of the Island of Lampedusa by a couple of hours or so. I found out this news much later. At the same time, and again, I read this in a newspaper a long time later, the naval party who landed on Linosa were immediately presented with a surrender and a note from a Spitfire pilot who reported that as a prisoner on the island, he had been treated very well and that he trusted that the islanders would be treated in the same manner.

The submarine motored along for some time, and then a klaxon sounded, hatches banged closed, and it dived down. Shortly afterwards, the motors stopped, and all was quiet. I presumed we were sitting on the seabed. I didn't fancy this at all. I lay on a bunk, cursed my bad luck, and felt all alone in the world again. What's the next move, I wondered.

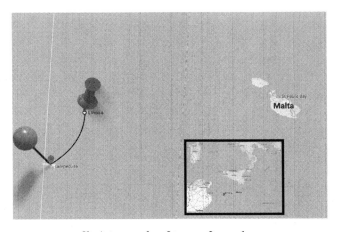

Ken's journey from Linosa to Lampedusa

Chapter 22

A Life Under the Ocean Waves

I suppose that everything had been stowed away and made shipshape, or whatever they do in the Navy, because, after a short while, three Officers joined me in the tiny Officers' Mess. There was the Captain, who spoke a little English, and the Second in Command, who I believe was the Engineer, and he spoke French. The third man was, I think, the Navigator. They were all remarkably pleasant and endeavoured to start some conversation. It was lovely and engaging, and I felt in no danger whatsoever. The Captain said I would now be shown the limits beyond which I must not attempt to go. The junior officer escorted me from the Mess a few yards to the toilet and wash basin. That's one problem solved, I thought. We returned to the Mess, and the Captain stood up and motioned me to follow him. We went in the opposite direction and into the Control Centre of the submarine. He showed me a place to sit, and I understood I should be able to sit there when the submarine motored along the surface at night. The seat was directly under a draught up to the conning tower, and at night, it was a tremendous relief to sit there in the strong down draught of cool, fresh air.

We then returned to the Mess, and dinner was served. The first course, of course, was pasta, and the Captain asked me if I knew what it was. "Yes," I said, "it's macaroni." He smiled at me and quietly said, "No, it's spaghetti." As you read this, it may sound strange, but I had never actually seen spaghetti before. I had eaten macaroni pudding many times at home, though. In the UK before World War II, there were no such things as Italian, Indian, or Chinese restaurants. The food in those days was strictly British!

Apart from the daily spaghetti meals, I recall nothing about the food on the submarine except that it was terrific, and the best I had experienced since being taken prisoner. I enjoyed it all. It was to be the best food I was to have for some considerable time to come.

The vessel was large and carried a crew of over fifty submariners. I hadn't thought much about submarines - to be fair, I hadn't thought about them at all. But it did seem to me to be a big crew. The routine on board soon became clear. They had been on a long voyage, and being now close to home and, I presume, some shore leave, they were intent on ensuring that nothing would happen to prevent them from reaching the harbour on mainland Italy.

About an hour before dawn, they would submerge and sit quietly on the sea bed until an hour after nightfall, when they would surface and motor along. The submarine did not move at all whilst submerged. This was June in the Mediterranean, and the days were fairly long. By the time we surfaced at night, everyone was virtually gasping for breath. It was awful, more so, I suppose, because I was not used to it. However, I was fit and young, so I survived.

Shortly after we surfaced each night, the Captain would come to the Mess and take me to my seat in the control room under the precious draught of fresh air. The crew members on duty would constantly check their instruments, and a sing-song would often be going on. I would be asked to join in and would do so to the very limited extent of my ability. The Captain told me I could smoke if I wished whilst sitting in the control room. This was a welcome deviation.

Some extraordinary things happened, so let me remind you that I was on an Italian submarine as their prisoner. Yet, the Officers and Crew accepted me as a welcome visitor. That had been my opinion of prisoner-of-war life so far, and I found it hard to believe. I have remarked before and I do so again, that the Italians are not a war-like people, and yet I suppose that if they had their backs to the wall, they would fight as remorsely as anyone else. However, here I was, and it became apparent that I was the only person aboard who possessed cigarettes. I started a daily rationing system. Looking back on this after fifty years, it still seems unbelievable. There was absolutely nothing, of course, to stop them from relieving me of the whole stock of cigarettes - and yet they did not. I always had faith in my stock of cigarettes as they could be used as collateral. And so I was proved right. I gave the Captain three cigarettes each morning and the Second in Command two cigarettes. Each evening during the lull in the sing-song, I laid two cigarettes on a table and motioned to the crew to play cards to see which two would win one cigarette each. It was a wonderful system and made relations very convivial. I took care not to smoke more than one myself. Amazingly, I taught them to sing "Run Rabbit, Run" and a couple of other songs I cannot recall.

So life was, for the time being, quite passable but boring, except for the attacks most days from ships or aircraft while we sat there on the sea bed. They certainly got very close with their depth charges, and the submarine was bashed onto its side more than once. But, thank God, they never had a direct hit. I cannot recall the exact length of the voyage, but I would estimate it to be over a week. I suppose nine or ten days, considering the distance involved. They didn't seem to care how long it took as long as they reached port safely.

During this voyage, the Engineer Officer told me that some time ago, he had been on a submarine that had climbed quite a way up the River Thames, and he seemed to be rightly proud of this achievement. He did not say, however, that they had attacked or sunk any vessels. It had occurred to me several times over the last few weeks that I was regarded as quite an important person for them to take all this trouble in making sure that I did not get back to my fellow men. I was undoubtedly the first enemy most of them had encountered, and I thought of the tale the submariners would have to tell their families when they got home! Probably the same as I am now, fifty years later, telling!

Whilst waiting one night to be invited into the control room, I took stock of my capital - cigarettes. I had enough for that night and two or three leftovers for myself. I resolved to tell them tonight. It was unbelievable, but I felt I had become their friend! I sat on my seat, and the night proceeded as usual until I was told to return to the Mess. But it didn't happen. The Captain came down the hatchway and confronted me. As usual, when he addressed me, I stood up out of respect for his position. After all, he was the Captain, and I was but a Prisoner of War on his ship. The Captain said that we should reach the harbour soon after it came light, and would I accompany him to the bridge (or, in this case, the conning tower) and take the salute. It was the custom that a ship of the Italian Navy, on reaching its home port, would be greeted with a gun salute. I said that I had not got a cap. It is a rule of the United Kingdom Forces that you must not salute - or return a salute if you are not correctly dressed - that is, wearing a complete uniform. However, I again decided to break the rules and accompany him. It was an interesting experience, especially after having spent so long below. A steward brought us coffee. This was indeed first-class treatment; of course, these were continental Italians who respected officer status - even that of the enemy.

Dawn came, and I saw land on the horizon within an hour. "Italia," said the Captain, and he told me we would land in Taranto. It was very enjoyable up there on the conning tower, watching the land come closer and closer and drinking another cup of their very strong, sweet coffee. Eventually, I could make out what appeared to be a fortress on either side of the harbour entrance, and again, the Captain pointed and said, "Taranto," and then it came again: "For you, the war is over." I wondered yet again what was in store for me. I had been extremely lucky so far.

Just before the submarine passed through the harbour entrance, the Captain motioned to me. I stood alongside him, and we both saluted and kept the salute until there was a returned two-gun salute. As soon as we had passed the entrance, he busied himself with orders to the crew below in the control room, and we slackened speed and approached a quayside.

As we tied up, the Captain told me to return to the Mess and stay there until he came for me. I sat there, thinking that he would be organising a guard. After about three-quarters of an hour, the Captain came into the Mess and handed me—guess what—a carton of two hundred cigarettes! I thanked him as sincerely as I could and followed him to the quayside, where he handed me over to two Army guards.

It had been an incredible voyage by submarine, and again, I remembered its name, but eventually, of course, it disappeared from my memory. It is a fair way from Lampedusa to Taranto in the heel of Italy, so, at the slow rate of progress, I suppose it may have been nearer ten days than a week. Anyway, they achieved their objective - to get safely home. Little did they, or I for that matter, know what would happen to them in the not-too-distant future. But I was a land-lubber once again.

Ken's journey by submarine

Chapter 23

Mainland Italy

We walked a short way to a building just off the quayside and went to the first floor. One of the guards opened a door and beckoned me to enter. The bedroom was quite spacious, housing a large bed, a table, a chair, and a wardrobe. One guard remained outside the door, and I was left to my own thoughts. I celebrated by having a cigarette. I still had a nice lighter I had bought way back during my three-day rest in Constantine. It seemed like years and years had passed since that time, so much had happened since then.

I was being kept in a seaplane Officer's Mess, although I never saw any pilots. The bedroom was ensuite, so I was alright for the necessities. Occasionally, the door would open, and the guard would enter. He would look all around the room to satisfy himself that I was not knocking holes in walls or anything, and then he would leave me again. He was a surly-looking chap, and I took an instant dislike to him.

Eventually, the door opened again, and in came a sort of steward bearing a tray with coffee, bread, and a plate of fried fish. This was the first time in my life that I had been served fish with their heads still on! But I was hungry and thoroughly enjoyed the meal. The three meals a day - if you call continental breakfast a meal - were the only diversion from what became a rather dull existence. Some kind soul had sent me a few Italian periodicals. I read and reread the Italian and began to recognise a few words. There were quite a few pictures of the great leader Mussolini, who, from the outset, had chosen the wrong side, and we all know what happened to him!

During the days that followed, I only have two incidents to report. Firstly, the bedroom door opened one day, and in came a person - or more correctly - a Catholic priest. I cannot remember which language formed the basis of the conversation, but it turned out that he was on a purely welfare visit. Was I well? Did I have sufficient food? Was I well treated? I reassured him on these points, and he said that if I gave him my Number, Rank, Name, and home address, he would do his best to get a message home via radio to my parents through the Vatican. As a Prisoner of War, one is obliged to give a Number, Rank, and Name, but absolutely no other information. However, he seemed to be a bona fide Member of the Cloth, so I gave him what he requested. He asked what message I would like to send. These details were, in fact, broadcast from the Vatican and picked up by a dedicated individual who took it upon himself to conduct this work of listening in and sending the messages on postcards to the concerned people. If I remember correctly, the postcard came from someone on the south coast of the UK. I think my mother received this message before she got an official letter from my Squadron Leader, but I am unsure about that point.

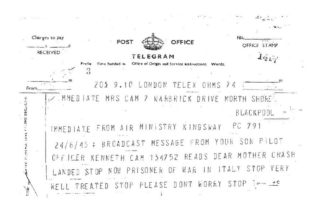

The second incident was an air raid on the harbour of Taranto. The Allies were starting their campaign on mainland Italy. Apart from the air raid, I knew nothing about how the war was going, but obviously, we were not doing too badly. I was told later that there was some quite fierce fighting to conquer Sicily, and after that, footholds were established on mainland Italy itself. But at the time, I knew little or, more truthfully, nothing of all this. I was still living a monk-like existence.

Back to the air raid on Taranto. The sirens sounded, and there was lots of shouting, screaming, and running about. My room door burst open, and the visual message from the guard needed little interpretation. We practically ran to an air raid underground shelter. The place was already bursting at the seams with dozens of civilians and military personnel, and the noise was unbelievable. Shouting, screaming, crying. People all around crossing themselves and praying loudly. How God was supposed to hear any supplication above the row was a mystery. I think that this may have been their first experience of war on their doorstep, but I was still conditioned to it, and consequently, it had little effect on me. Then, a strange thing happened. After a time, this sort of mad panic began to rub off, so much so that I bellowed at the top of my voice several times. "Silencio, silencio!" Suddenly, there was quiet, and most turned in my direction.

I motioned to keep quiet, and incredibly, they did. Thinking of it later, I suppose they could have turned on me, and I would have been a goner! But not so, and the rest of the raid passed in quiet prayer. An officer had joined my guard - perhaps he was there to ensure that I didn't make a run for it. However, during this quiet, he looked at me and smiled, and I shrugged my shoulders and smiled back. Don't forget, I was the enemy and, therefore, was, in their eyes, responsible for this upset in their lives.

The "all clear" sounded, and we returned to my quarters. The guard unlocked the door of my room and practically shoved me inside. The air raid had obviously upset him, and the sight of my lighter and cigarettes was too much for him to bear. He walked over to my table and, keeping one eye on me, proceeded to secrete the lighter and cigarettes about his person. I protested as best I could, but it was to no avail. They were gone forever. Very distressing, and I cursed him. I must apologise again for not remembering exactly how long I stayed in this "accommodation". Still, shortly after the air raid, I was awakened early one morning and found myself in the company of an Officer and a Corporal. I gathered my belongings, which took about ten seconds, and we left the building. That was the last of Taranto.

Chapter 24

Train Journey Number One

The three of us set off to walk, and as we passed odd groups of early risers, all eyes were upon me. They pointed at us and conversed among themselves. It was like being a well-known film star, but the circumstances were somewhat different!

We arrived at a railway station and boarded a train. Although the train was packed, we had a compartment to ourselves, which was a blessing. I have called this chapter "Train Journey Number One" because it was the first of several, and looking back on them, it was undoubtedly the most comfortable. I knew that as an Officer Prisoner of War, I was entitled under the Geneva Convention to a certain amount of money, depending on my rank, per day. I started pestering the officer to pass some cash over to me. He was nonplussed about this demand, but some hours later, due to my persistence, he handed over some cash! I knew not how much I had been given, but what I did know was that I was determined to spend it at the first available opportunity - preferably on something to eat. It appeared that, as in other countries involved in a war, train journeys were lengthy and slow.

When I needed to use the toilet, I communicated this to the officer. He dispatched the Corporal, who came back after a few minutes and escorted me to the cabinet. This was another of those dreadful "holes in the floor." The door of the toilet was left open, and he stood fairly and squarely in it, facing me, his rifle at the ready until I had finished—a procedure which I was to get accustomed to in the future.

We returned to the compartment, and I just sat and watched the countryside go by. Eventually, we arrived and stopped at a station, and the officer informed me that we were in Naples. Again, the big question loomed in my mind. Where were we going, and what were we going for? It was a state of affairs one never got used to. However, it turned out that we had to wait for another train for two or three hours, and the officer and I sat on a bench seat, while the Corporal stood behind us. How can I spend some money? I thought. How can I get something to eat?

A barrow boy arrived and took up his position some fifty yards away. His barrow seemed to be full of fruit of some sort, and my immediate problem was solved. I asked the officer as best as I could and pointed to the barrow. He agreed, and we walked over. Apparently, they were apricots - but I had never seen an apricot in the raw - I'd only ever known them in tins. However, now wasn't the time to question this. I shoved all my money into the fellow's hand, and he gave me three big bags full of the fruit in exchange. We returned to the bench seat, and I gazed in wonderment at my new acquisition. I'll never get through all these, I thought, so I gave one bag to the officer to be shared with his Corporal. This was greatly appreciated, and we all ate in silence.

The time came, and we boarded a train. When we were on our way, I was told that our next destination was Rome. We changed trains again to continue our journey into the unknown. After a couple of hours, the train stopped at a small countryside station and we got off. I looked at the station name, and to the best of my memory, it read Merriot Poggiot or something like that. Outside the station, our transport waited. To those who know, this vehicle was one of the original Fiat Cinquecento, a tiny car! It was an open-topped vehicle, and we piled in. With the three of us and a driver, it was extremely uncomfortable—the driver and the officer in the front seats, and the Corporal and I in the back. Talk about sardines! Where to next?

The poor little engine laboured as we climbed into the hills and eventually arrived at a building resembling a Monastery. And so it was, for the time being, that this turned out to be the journey's end. I was piloted along a stone-floored corridor and ushered into a cell. It contained a bed, chair, and table, as usual. My new Home!

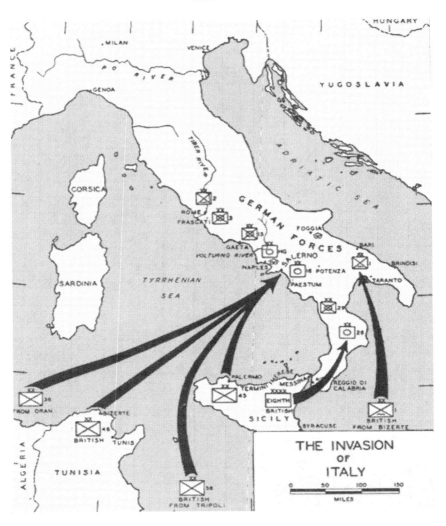

Chapter 25

Solitary Confinement

I surveyed my new surroundings, which didn't take very long at all. On the table was a book, some kind soul had left it, and it was written in English, which was something new, and I appreciated the gesture. It appeared to be a love story novel, and I put it aside for the time being, lay on the bed, and tried to sleep. The words solitary confinement have a wealth of meaning, but I was, by now, getting accustomed to it - if one ever does.

The door clanged open, and in came a guard bearing a tray containing some soup-like pasta, bread, and an item I had never encountered before. It was a piece of about two cubic inches of cheese, as hard as a rock. I immediately took to the taste and have liked it very much ever since. It was parmesan, and after the pasta and bread, I nibbled at it sparingly. This ration of cheese came up every night, and I thoroughly enjoyed it.

At times, I heard voices along the corridor that told me I was not the only occupant in the cells. I had plenty of time over the last couple of months to meditate, and it appeared to me that I had arrived in the correct place for such mental activity. I also gleaned from the voices the information I required concerning the toilet arrangements. The toilet facilities play an important part in life, but for the British, unlike the continentals, these duties should be carried out in private. Those days, I am afraid, had gone. The system was simple: one banged on the cell door and shouted "cabinetto" until a response was received from the guard. He provided an escort to the end of the corridor past the other cells, and again, there was the hole in the floor - no doubt hygienic, but it did take a bit of getting used to, especially as the guard again stood in the doorway and watched the procedure. These trips, along with the meals provided, were the only respite from the monotonous routine. Somewhere along the line, my twenty-second birthday came and went, and after I had been in my new surroundings for a few days, I was taken to the Commandant's palatial office to be interviewed.

There he sat behind a big desk, resplendent in his beautiful uniform. The Captain was polite to an excess, immediately putting one on guard. I understood that this was an interrogation place, and after establishing my Number, Rank, and Name, he proceeded (in English) to ask questions about my squadron and the like. All of which I refused to answer. In consequence, he offered me a cigarette. This was very tempting, but when I examined it and saw that it was a Player's (a very famous British cigarette brand) with the words "British Red Cross" printed alongside, I threw it back across the desk to him, and asked him how he came to have what belonged rightly to his prisoners. This abruptly ended the interview, and he was angry that I had adopted such an attitude, sending me back to my cell. I could have done with a smoke too!

I read the book several times, but the love story merely told me that nobody loved me at that time, and I was still rather alone in this precarious life. Gazing at the ceiling whilst lying on my bed, I saw it was painted white with several rows of large diamonds painted in red. Eventually, I noticed that one of the red diamonds, about four inches long, differed slightly from the rest. Why was this? What was it?

I knew the guard would open the flap in the door and look through the spy hole every so often to see what the inmate was up to, so I chose my time and put the table on top of the bed and the chair on top of the table. I climbed up, now able to touch the diamond, and discovered that it was made of a pliable canvas material. "A hidden microphone!" I thought. So, I thought about my next move.

Again, by placing the chair on the table and positioning it against the outer wall, I could see through the small barred opening and watch the military playing boules in the evening. When they played boules the following evening, I got up to the diamond and pulled back the canvas. There it was — a microphone. I yanked it from its connections and returned my furniture to the position by the window. I took aim, launched the microphone between the bars, and saw it land on their boules court. What a shock they got. It was wonderful. I revelled in it. But not for long.

The cell door clanged open, and I was shoved along the corridor and into the Commandant's room. He was blazing. "Not this chap again," I could see him thinking. The interview was short; he gave me another seven days of solitary confinement. But secretly, I was well pleased with the episode, and I thought that seven days would pass quickly. At least that's what I thought. It was a tedious wait, and I began to rue my indiscretion somewhat.

However, as I think about it years later, it still seems like a good idea. It helps to keep spirits up. But the memory of these things lingers in the mind. After all, if they didn't, then I would have nothing to write about. I tried all sorts of mental activities to while away the time. I assessed the measurement of the span of my outstretched hand between thumb and little finger and endeavoured to measure the size of a wall. Then I mentally calculated the area of one wall, followed by the floor, which was also the size of the ceiling, and so on, until I reached the stage of trying to multiply and arrive at the volume of the cell. I then attempted to calculate the areas of the bed, table, and so on and so on.

The seven days dragged on, and on the eighth day, after breakfast, I was told to gather my kit and follow the guard. It was a real treat to get outside the prison walls, and once again, I was told to get into the Fiat 500 with my officer and Corporal guards. Back down the lanes to the railway station. The usual questions came to mind. Where were we going, and for what purpose? We stood on the station platform for a while before boarding the train. We went back to Rome and waited again for another train. They say that everything comes to those who wait, and of course, it did; and again, we boarded a train. There was little to no conversation, and try as I might, I could not find out our destination.

It was a long journey, and I remember going through a tunnel. The train stopped many times, and I occupied myself by watching the scenery pass by and trying to read the station names, but I couldn't glean much from this exercise. Eventually, we got off the train at a place called Modena. That meant nothing to me either. We climbed into the back of a lorry, which set off immediately. The lack of information about my destination was beginning to worry me. At some distance out of town, the truck stopped, and we dismounted. What did I see? The main gates of what appeared to be an established prison camp. We entered the guard room, and I was officially handed over to the Camp Commandant, who promptly signed a receipt for me. My railway journey guards departed, and I stood before the officer. He looked at me and again pronounced what I had heard several times over the last couple of months - "For you, the war is over". The door opened, and in came a chap who was obviously a Prisoner of War. He welcomed me and shook hands. Meeting a fellow prisoner was a real treat, and my spirits soared. It was the first time since my crash landing that I met someone on our side of the war.

Chapter 26

My New Life

With my new friend, I left the guard room and walked across the central parade ground, which was surrounded by well-built barrack-type buildings. It appeared that my companion was a captain of the South African Forces and had been captured in the region of Tobruk. He said that life here was not too bad and there was no maltreatment. Good news indeed!

On the way across the parade ground, my guide quickly informed me that Sicily had been conquered and that fighting was now well established on the mainland. There was indeed German resistance, as one would imagine, but overall, the war against the enemy was progressing favourably.

We entered a room that had been designated as the senior British Officers' Quarters and office, and two officers confronted me. As I sat down, they proceeded to assure themselves that I was a bona fide British Officer - and I was then asked to tell my story to date. As soon as I had finished summarising my travels since Linosa, they were convinced that I was who I claimed to be. Then we all stood up, and there were handshakes and a hearty welcome. A cup of coffee was produced, and I was told about my new accommodation, the Modena Campo Di Prigioniera Di Guerra. It would appear that after completing my somewhat lonely apprenticeship, I had now sort of "passed out" and had suddenly become a fully fledged Prisoner of War. What a qualification!

The three officers in the room, together with the great majority of the prisoners, were South African Army personnel. I was told that RAF prisoners were extremely few and far between, and they were probably right, as I cannot accurately remember meeting any in the camp.

I was taken to one of the barrack buildings and given a spare bed about a quarter of the way down the building from the door. The buildings were all the same; they were made of concrete with marble flooring and windows down each side. In the centre was a big tiled stufa, or stove, for winter use. Compared with the accommodation I was to experience over the next couple of years, these were quite palatial. There was a good yard between each bed, and the beds were not stacked one on top of the other. I wondered how cold or warm the coming winter months would be and whether there would be enough fuel for the stove.

The town of Modena is approximately 40 miles from Bologna in northeastern Italy, and although it is well south of the Alps, I thought it might get rather chilly. I asked my new acquaintances questions to establish whether I could get more clothing. I still had only shoes, socks, underpants, shorts, and a shirt. One chap said, "I'll get you some," and off he went. About an hour later, he returned with a shirt, trousers, and socks. I was most grateful and told him so. "We're all in this boat together," he remarked. There was a fair sprinkling of British Officers in the barracks allocated to me, which, I presume, is why I was sent there.

Over the next few days, the camp routine became clear. There was a parade, and a count of all prisoners was taken twice a day. The meals were served from a cookhouse. You had your own plate, cup, and dixie, and most meals consisted of bread and a watery soup with pieces of pasta and vegetables floating about in it. Hardly cordon bleu, but at least it kept one alive, which is all one could expect from the enemy. I quickly began to lose the feeling of loneliness that I had experienced since landing in Linosa, and a camaraderie soon developed.

Announcements were made about the Allies' progress in Italy, and there had been further landings on the West Coast.

Maintaining a strong sense of hope is vital to a Prisoner of War, and news items—especially good news items—were essential to one's well-being. I was told that most of the British prisoners taken in the North Africa campaign, mainly in the Western Desert, were in a large camp at Bari on the south Adriatic coast of Italy.

I have titled this chapter in the story "My New Life", and so it was. The previous months of isolation were apparently behind me, and I now felt much more secure—if one can feel secure in such circumstances. I told myself it was a matter of settling down and waiting for the war to end. If I were fortunate enough to get through that far, then when fighting ceased, I would do everything possible to get myself home. In other words, I would look after myself above all else. I would escape - if the chance came - but I certainly was not going to stick my neck out. The reader may call those thoughts somewhat cowardly, be that as it may, but the proof of the pudding is that after fifty-five years, I am still here!

I did have concerns: How long will it be before this war ends? Will I be here for months or years? However, being in the company of other fellows made things so much easier.

Rumours were, of course, rife and at least provided talking points. Still, one day, around the middle of September 1943, the unbelievable news came into the camp that the Italians had signed a secret Armistice with the Allies and deserted their German Allies. The next twenty-four hours were impossible to describe. Was it true? Were we to be freed? Were we to be sent home? Although we all paraded at the usual time, there was no count. We were addressed by the Senior Officer of the camp, who informed us that the Italians had, in fact, packed it in, and although the guards might disappear, it was our duty to remain in the camp until he had been able to negotiate arrangements. The guards did, in fact, disappear, shortly followed by some POWs. Within a very short time, a matter of a few hours, the Italian guards were replaced by other guards, but unfortunately, not of the same nationality.

These new guards were German! A vastly different kettle of fish indeed! It was immediately very clear to see that these lads meant business. Gone were the rather pleasant, peace-loving Italians, and in came the brutally Efficient Huns who obviously would stand no messing about. Over the next few days, prisoners who had taken the opportunity to escape during the interim period were escorted back into the camp individually. Perhaps a few did get clear and were lucky enough to find shelter and food, and wait until the war passed them by. Things began to happen very quickly, and we found ourselves being marched out of the camp in parties of about one hundred. The usual questions came to mind - where now and for what?

Chapter 27

On the Move Again

Although the Italians had given up the struggle, it did not mean that all fighting in Italy stopped, far from it. The Germans carried on as usual, and many Italians were rounded up and transported to Germany as forced labour.

We arrived at the railway station, not to see a train composed of railway carriages, but a train of closed cattle trunks. I am sure you have seen them, eight horses or forty men, it said on the side of the truck, and that's what they did. They counted forty into each car, and that ominous sound returned - the door clanged shut. There was a small grilled window near the roof on opposite sides of the truck. We all felt miserable. We could hear the sound of other doors closing down the train, and after a few hours, the train set off.

I suppose this was train Journey number three, and the quality of accommodation was decidedly third class or below. There was no room to lie down, so everyone sat hunched up. A back-to-back position soon became the most comfortable posture. Progress was very slow indeed, and the train would stop frequently for long periods. Toilet facilities were, of course, nonexistent. You will wonder, perhaps, how a bunch of civilised men behaved in such circumstances—so I will explain. Odd containers appeared from the prisoners' belongings and were used as receptacles for waste matter from their bodies. In the case of urine, one launched it through the grill in one of the small openings, and all those nearby moved out of the way during this procedure to avoid coming into contact with the liquid. In the case of solid materials, I am afraid that the only method of dealing with them was to carefully handle them and push them through the grill piece by piece. I have mentioned toilet facilities several times during these writings and apologise for doing so, but they are fundamentally important, especially in such awful circumstances.

Life within the confines of the cattle trucks was, to say the least, unexpected. In hindsight, it was awful, and I would not wish it upon anyone. Since the war, one has seen many films about the transportation of Jews from all parts of German-occupied territories to extermination camps, and I suppose I am one of the comparatively few people who can imagine and understand the feelings of those involved. Thank God our destination was not the same as that of the unfortunate. It was terrible for men, let alone women and children; however, back to our plight on the way from Italy to Germany.

On our train, we were the second of several trains of prisoners to be transported. On the first trainload, the guards were German, but as most prison guards were second— or third—class soldiers, they were not particularly fit for the front line due to their physical and age limitations. I was told later that some two hundred prisoners escaped one way or another from that train, although I do not know how many attained actual and lasting freedom. I don't suppose there were many. I only knew one such British soldier who did so, and he managed to get somehow into Switzerland, where he was interned for the remainder of the war. This mass escape was frowned upon by the German Authorities, and so the method of our second train was altered. Quite simply, the guards were replaced, and the SS troops took over the job. These troops were mean and tough and thought little of ending one's life at the drop of a hat, and there are words to describe such people - but I shall leave them for you to decide.

After a few days and nights, the train made one of its frequent stops, and the truck door was pulled back. The fresh air was like an immediate tonic, and we were told to get out. I assume they believed this would be a toilet stop. What they thought we were supposed to have been doing since we boarded the train—goodness knows! At intervals along the line of cattle trucks was a flat truck with a couple of machine guns and four soldiers. At a previous stop, one prisoner was caught sawing the floorboards of the car and was dragged out and, bound up with barbed wire, flung onto a flat truck and left to die. Each truckload of prisoners was taken to view the lad, and the message was obvious. If you try to escape, that will be your fate! I never heard of anyone else trying to get out.

We climbed back into our trucks, and before the door was closed, a German slung in a crate of apples. This was the first food we had seen. Did we relish it?! The same old questions kept resurfacing in my mind, time and time again. Where to? And what for?

The journey dragged on and on until we eventually arrived in Innsbruck, Austria, where we experienced the most humiliating and degrading episode of the entire trip. It has been said before, and I do not apologise for saying it here, that there are several traits of character which are peculiar to the British. It is, of course, those traits of character that make one nation different from the next. And long may it remain so. I am speaking of a particular dogged determination that results in not knowing when one is beaten. In these circumstances, one lives on a certain amount of hope and keeps plodding on. Perhaps the reader may not fully understand what I am getting at, and if I cannot express my thoughts and memories explicitly, then I am sorry.

We were marched from the railway sidings in parties of two trucks at a time through the station and out into a main street of Innsbruck. Again, it is evident that the SS boys meant business, and arguing or disobeying would have been very foolish. We were lined up in a single file and marched along the gutter. When halted, the order was barked out to lower our trousers and squat in the gutter. The German word of command came, which resembles a four-letter English word that, in polite terms, means to evacuate the bowel. Complete and utter ignominy and humiliation! Austrian and other passers-by would grin and spit at us, and some would go as far as to kick us. I expect that to stand up and disobey the order would have meant immediate death. All things, one way or another, come to an end. And so did this awful trial. We were marched back to our trucks.

Many years later, I was on a motoring holiday with Betty and went to the street and the railway station. It was so well etched into my memory that I had no difficulty finding the location.

We were provided with food and water in our trucks, but I don't recall what it was. The next halt was in a goods yard somewhere, and we spent a night there alongside another train of cattle trucks. Those were filled with Italians who were being transported to Germany as forced labour. For some reason best known to others, their truck doors remained open. The Italian occupants of the truck opposite us used a suitcase as a toilet, and they decided that, as this receptacle was now full, they would discard it out of the door. Unfortunately, it landed and burst immediately next to our truck, and the stench all night was indescribable. Was this life in the raw - or was it not?

The next port of disembarkation was a vast, well-established prison camp called Moosburg, located in Bavaria. As you can imagine, we were all extremely glad to be out of the trucks and found ourselves in a large hut with three-tier bunks, of which you have no doubt seen pictures. We were all absolutely dead tired and welcomed our new accommodation!

Chapter 28

Moosburg - Fort Bismark - Weinburg - Sagan

The heading of this chapter may read like a holiday brochure describing a tour. However, it is the best way I could think of to describe the following weeks.

Moosburg was a large—very large—camp that had been established for several years. I imagine it housed prisoners of various nationalities. There were British, American, French, Russian, and men from European countries such as Czechoslovakia, Poland, Hungary, and the like. It was probably the nearest to what were known as concentration camps that I ever experienced. Some political prisoners had been incarcerated before 1939, when the British became involved in the war.

I was one day walking past the solitary confinement or punishment block when I heard prisoners shouting in an endeavour to converse with any passerby. I shouted back to a chap who was an American and hungry for any news about the war's progress. One had to be very careful when doing something like this - it was dangerous to upset any walkabout guards. The penalty for any such action was to find oneself in a cell immediately. I quickly learned to keep a low profile at all times. The degradation of my last train journey was still fresh in my mind and remains so to this day.

Back at our arrival place, I chose a top bunk and climbed up to find that the wooden bed was a mass of insects of many types—a terrible sight. However, as I said, I was dog tired, so I dragged my arm and hand across the surface and swept off as many as possible. I still had the blanket I had brought from the camp at Modena, so I spread it out and lay on top of it. I immediately fell asleep and was awakened by a guard shouting and bawling, "Raus Raus!" which politely means "Get out". We all assembled outside and were put in charge of a Frenchman who was appreciably older than us and was obviously a "trustee". He was one of those long-standing political prisoners. We were on our way to be "fed".

"Frenchy," as we soon began to call him, was in charge of our hut, and each day when he came to get us, we said to him: "What's for dinner, Frenchy?" The reply was the same every time: "Zowp," he said - and that is what it was - a very watery soup with odd bits of vegetables, mainly cabbage, floating about, plus a hunk of black bread. It is strange to think of it now, but whenever you left your bed, you took all your possessions - empty tins, blanket, dixie - whatever you had. They were like gold! It goes without saying that if you didn't have a receptacle, you simply didn't get any "Zowp!" The old saying "You look after yourself in life" was certainly true.

It is not a matter of being able to trust one's fellow men, regardless of nationality, but in circumstances like these, survival is survival.

It was excellent news to find out that we would not have to stay at this camp for very long, perhaps just a week or ten days, as it was apparent that they were sorting prisoners into different categories. They included, but were not limited to, rank, nationality, and political ideology. One morning, we said our farewell to Frenchy and departed for the station.

I prayed that it would not be more of the cattle truck business, and my prayers were answered. They were extremely old and small railway carriages, and the whole train seemed to be wrapped in barbed wire with extra bars across the windows and doors. Comparatively, it was luxury. We boarded and trundled off. This was a much smaller lot of prisoners, perhaps a couple of hundred. The feeling was unanimous: We were all extremely glad to see the back of Moosburg.

And now, memory completely fails me regarding the next prison. Was it Fort Bismarck, or was it Weinburg? It does not matter, as I shall seek to describe each place. I have chosen Fort Bismarck to be the next place. This is situated, I think, at a place called Offenburg, which is east of Strasbourg on the German side of the German/Alsace border. In mentioning different camps, let me explain that "Stalag" means camp or prison, "Oflag" is a camp for Officers, "Marleg" is a camp for naval personnel, and "Stalag Luft" is a camp for aircrews.

Fort Bismarck was built in the shape of a flattened arrowhead with a deep but dry moat on the forward side of the arrowhead and solid earth along the back side. Guards constantly patrolled along the top of the moat and could, therefore, see both the moat itself and the fort. However, as the moat was angled, if they were stationed at the far end of the wall, the other end was out of sight. There was always some activity in the moat, and of course, the odd diversions were set up to keep the guard's attention in one direction whilst an escape was actually in progress up the other end.

I witnessed this only once, and the two escapees climbed nearly to the top of the moat wall before being spotted. They were escorted to the main guardhouse in the centre of the moat wall. I know nothing about their fate. We were no longer in the hands of the SS Troops, which made life a little more pleasant - if there was any pleasure at all. But everything is a matter of degree - is it not? I think I have only one more comment about Fort Bismarck, where our stay was once again short. And that remark concerns the beds. The rooms were located below ground level and were very long and narrow, with only one bed. It was a sort of sloping shelf, some six feet from front to back, and stretched the length of the room. Thus, the "bed" housed about thirty prisoners. I never saw that arrangement of sleeping again, but then we were never housed in a fort again.

The next journey was again in the old passenger carriages, prompting no comment other than to remind the reader of the constant uncertainty about our new destination and the reason for it.

Food was always a significant problem and was mainly non-existent while travelling. Odd prisoners became sick, and some quite ill, but there was nothing we could do except shout for a guard at the first opportunity. Sometimes, they were dealt with, and other times, they were not.

Our journey ended at an established camp called Weinburg. This was a brief journey, and I presume it was intended to separate those of

Officer rank. It was Oflag VA. The established routine of camp life was beginning to reappear. Two roll calls, or more accurately, head counts, daily. There are two essential items here that warrant comment.

Firstly, on a sunny afternoon, we all turned our heads skyward as the sound of an aircraft approached. Suddenly, they were spotted - a large formation of what appeared to be American bombers (the B-29 or Flying Fortress). This prompted loud cheers, which were silenced by a guard in a guard box letting off a long burst from his machine gun. We were all thrilled, and although the planes were relatively high, we were convinced our guess was correct. We learned later that it had been a daylight bombing raid on a ball-bearing factory at Schweinfurt.

Typical UK Red Cross food parcel during the Second World War

The second item was even better news! It was the first time I saw (and was given a half share) in a British Red Cross Food parcel. Absolutely wonderful! I simply cannot describe the utter feeling of joy and elation to you. The Red Cross Food parcels were each about ten pounds in weight and were sent by the British, Canadian, Australian & New Zealand, and later the American Red Cross, and varied a little in their contents. In the British parcel were such items as hard biscuits, sultanas, sardines, boiled bacon, sugar, condensed milk, dried egg, and sometimes fifty cigarettes - all these items were tinned. Tea or cocoa was sometimes included, along with tinned margarine. All the parcels came from various countries to Switzerland, which then took upon itself the duty of distributing them as best it could around the various prison camps. Hence, the supply was highly irregular. Ideally, I think each prisoner was supposed to receive a parcel every month, or perhaps every two weeks - I am not sure.

What is more, I knew from my experience in the Italian interrogation monastery that some went astray! I should think that quite a lot fell into the wrong hands. Anyway, they were certainly lifesavers in the truest sense of the word.

Again, we enjoyed Weinburg's decent washing facilities, including showers, although the hours of water supply were restricted, and hot water was non-existent. "What did you expect?" I hear you say!

Our stay here was again short, and once again, some of us were on the move. We had all been given a metal tag bearing our name and official Prisoner of War Number. This was never to be removed from its string and was to be worn around the neck—on pain of death!

We were now well into the last quarter of 1943, and our final train journey brought us to Stalag Luft III. This camp was for aircrew personnel only and was, so we heard, absolutely escape-proof. It was built in the usual style, in an area cleared of the pine forests. It consisted of four compounds. The centre compound was for other ranks. The North Compound, where I was, was for British and Commonwealth Officers. The West Compound was reserved for Americans, while the East Compound housed the administration and hospital areas. I think I have got those correct, although it matters not. I suppose that we were a party of about forty or so. We marched from the railway station in the small town of Sagan to the front gates of Stalag Luft III. Masses of erections of barbed wire confronted us. Through the gates, we went to the forelager* between two lots of barbed wire fences and stopped to be treated like sheep once again - and counted. Knowing something of the German mentality, I suppose someone signed for us.

---

* In WWII military slang, particularly among British or Commonwealth forces, a "forelager" referred to an advance camp or forward maintenance area. It comes from the German word "Vorlager" (meaning "forward camp" or "outpost"), but English-speaking soldiers adapted and spelt it "forelager."

Chapter 29

Stalag Luft III - Sagan

Like in previous camps, news travels like lightning, and as we stood there, we saw a little crowd of prisoners assembling at the inner front gate, ready to greet the new intake and search the faces to see if there was anyone they knew. They were all eager for the latest war news, but we were not yet allowed to mingle with them. A Squadron Leader escorted us to a hut with a large room, and we were asked to wait there while we were interviewed individually to assess whether we were bona fide Air Force personnel. That over, the officer gave us a brief talk about the essentials of camp life, and then each of us was allocated a hut and a room number. Volunteers were standing by to show us our huts - mine was hut number 106 - but I forget the room number, although it was about halfway along. I went in, and as it happened, all five occupants were present at the time, and introductions were made.

I had landed on my feet because they were exceptionally well organised, as organised as a Prisoner of War can be. This was because they were all long-standing prisoners. And so we swapped experiences. Bob Coste - a Canadian who came to the UK in the mid-1930s and joined the RAF on a short commission (usually for five years). Coste was caught up in the war, as were the other short-service pre-war pilots in the room. Digger Young, an Australian, and a chap called Ian Cross were the only

MAKE IT DO

Squadron Leaders, the latter the son of Air Vice Marshal Cross. Mickey Rooney was a pilot of the Fleet Air Arm and hailed from Wigan. I cannot remember whether he was a short-service or a permanent member of the Fleet Air Arm. The fifth chap was a Frenchman called Peronne, who came from Paris and had escaped from the French Air Force around the time of Dunkirk and had managed to get to England and was taken into the RAF All five of them were shot down early in 1940, except Peronne who was late 1940. They had been prisoners for about three years when I joined them.

They were intelligent, sane, and sensible, which helped a great deal and made me feel welcome without being overly effusive. Again, I was fortunate to get the last bunk in their room. They had been in various prison camps over the years, and Stalag Luft III was a comparatively new camp. If I remember, two or three of my new roommates had suffered manacled* for periods, a distressing procedure which, thank God, I never had to experience. Bob Coste, Digger Young, and Ian Cross had all been operating on the Wellington Bombers. Peronne had been performing some special mission in a light aircraft over France, and Mickey Rooney was shot down somewhere around Calais whilst on some bombing trip in a light bomber called a Fairey Battle. This was a single-engined lumbering aircraft which, I am sure, you could overtake on a bike! You were just a sitting duck, very much like the Fleet Air Arm Swordfish. I was speaking to a naval man a couple of years ago, and I mentioned the business of going to war in a plane like the Battle and Swordfish. He remarked that the present-day Helicopter could fly faster backwards! Such is war, and such was the unprepared state that the UK found itself in the early stages. In fact, a friend in the pre-war Territorial Army was trained and prepared to go to war on horseback, armed with a

North Compound, Stalag Luft II. Sagan, Germany.

---

* Prisoners were sometimes shackled at the wrists, often as retaliation or punishment, making daily life extremely difficult and psychologically distressing.

sword. Thank God, I was a bit better off than that, although I ended up in the same place.

So, these were my new surroundings for the next period of my life. But - for how long? I shall try to describe life in my new abode as well as I can, and to that end, I have made many notes of events and feelings, but not necessarily in any order of time, until I left the place in January 1945.

The German word for prisoners of war is "Kriegsgefangene" (the Germans love these long words), so "Kriegies" was what we called ourselves. Germans were called "Goons". An "Appell" was a parade to be counted. A "Ferret" was a Goon who spent his time nosing around everywhere and everything to find items that could be used in a potential escape plan. There was an expert and dedicated Ferret we called "Rubberneck", who was very proficient at his job, but although he may have thought it, he was not infallible. A "Tame Goon" was a German guard who had been bribed and blackmailed into bringing precious articles into the camp, such as radio parts, identity cards, travel permits, and various items used in an escape or to be copied by our forger. A "snuffle hunt" was a search and tracker dog (usually an Alsatian) that patrolled endlessly, day and night. "Gen" was a long-standing term in the Services, and hence, there was "Pukka Gen" (reliable and accurate news) and "Duff Gen" (untrue news). There are undoubtedly more words; some may occasionally appear in the writings. As you may imagine, a Kreigie language had developed, and various accents evolved. I was guilty of speaking in a peculiar fashion and was not proud of it on my return home, but fortunately, I soon lost it when I came down to earth. Camp time was an hour ahead of German time, and they recognised this. So we arose at 8:00 am instead of 7:00 am, and lights out was at 10:00 pm, not 9:00 pm.

The German Camp Commandant was, by all reports, a more gentlemanly and kindly soul than the Nazi Party members and the Gestapo would have liked him to be. They saw their opportunity to relieve him of his post after the "Great Escape," which comes later in the tale. His adjutant was another strict but inoffensive soul called Pieber, a Captain responsible for the two daily counts in all the compounds. He wrote a book about his job in the camp after the war. He described the Americans as men who swaggered around constantly spitting and swearing, the British as reserved and who occupied themselves by quietly getting on with their escape plans, and the Dutch as trying to be more British than the British. Anyway, those were his impressions.

The Senior British Officer (SBO) was a Group Captain who was somewhat older than the typically young aircrew. He had a desk job in a Group Headquarters of the Bomber Command, and to give him his due, he was determined to experience exactly what a night bombing raid was like. He, therefore, went, one night, on a bombing raid and, unfortunately, very unfortunately for him, was shot down. I can imagine how he cursed his luck. However, he did learn firsthand what he was sending the lads out to do each night. He had to wait until the end of the war to relate his experience, which rather defeated the object of the exercise. He was a nice chap whom I met on a couple of occasions. He had the privilege of a room to himself, which was a mixed blessing. The SBO was the primary link with the Camp Commandant, with whom he had numerous meetings, during which he did his best to present any sincere objections the Kreigies had, as far as possible. We understood that there was as good a relationship as possible between them.

Friedrich Wilhelm von Lindeiner-Wildau. Stalag Luft III Commandant

There was an Escape Committee comprised of dedicated escapees, mainly fellows who were well-experienced in prison life. They called themselves "X," and they were pretty powerful. If a member came into your room to demand a bar of chocolate from a Red Cross parcel, a shirt suitable for dyeing, a bedboard, or whatever, he would mention "X," which was his authority. Many departments constantly worked in secret - forgers, map makers, tailors, dyers, and just about every trade you could imagine. All were doing their part to promote escapes. Miners, surveyors, joiners. I even met a chap who was a cat burglar before becoming a navigator. The list was endless. A Kreigie called French-Mullins, nicknamed "Efffie," had aspirations to take the Cloth, as they say, so he conducted a short Church service every day, to which all were welcome. Although I attended a couple of times, there never seemed to be a large congregation.

Goons were on duty daily and would enter rooms at any old time. On some of these occasions, the member of "X" would bribe a Goon with highly prized chocolate and cigarettes. Once the Goon had accepted a "gift," he was in real trouble, and if he was reported to the Commandant's Office as being guilty of such an offence, he was threatened by a transfer to the Russian Front. None wanted that, so they were in trouble from both sides. This "Goon-baiting," as it was called, was quite productive as far as the communal good was concerned and produced all sorts of helpful equipment.

The high double-barbed wire fencing was quite formidable, and there were often sentry boxes on stilts, which Goons constantly manned with machine guns. At some twenty feet inside the main fence was a single wire about one foot high. It was known as the trip wire, and if one crossed that without permission from the sentry, you were fired upon. Permission, therefore, was always sought to collect a ball and the like. In large clearings, the pine forest soil in which the prison camp was built consisted entirely of whitish sand, underlain by a thin layer of slightly darker soil. This made the disposal of sand excavated from the escape tunnels complicated. Still, when a theatre was built (mainly by the prisoners), a sloping floor was included ostensibly to give audiences a better view, but it was destined to become a home for white sand - and this worked remarkably well. The transportation of sand in sausage-shaped bags, secreted down the trouser leg, continued even during theatre performances, which Officer Goons always attended. Part of a row of seats towards the back of the theatre was set to one side, thus revealing steps for the sand carriers to get below and dump their loads.

Although the entire camp housed some 12,000 aircrew prisoners, our compound (the North) had around 1,400. In this theatre, a couple of prisoners began their acting careers and became well-known in plays and films after the war. They were both Fleet Air Arm Pilots. Firstly, Rupert (or Pud) Davies came to fame in the TV series "Inspector Maigret", and the second was Peter Butterworth, who was in many British films, including the "Carry On" series. Other budding actors didn't climb as high in the acting profession. An orchestra of about ten chaps played instruments donated by the Red Cross. For these Kreigies involved in the production of plays and shows, it was an ideal way to pass the time, and for those of us who were merely part of the audience, it provided excellent entertainment. Where costumes were necessary or desirable, those would be made from a fantastic arrangement of materials in the "Tailor's Shop", whose primary job was making civilian-type clothing and perhaps the odd German uniform, for escape purposes. The rule for escapees was that if you were caught whilst dressed as a German soldier, there was no question about it. You were considered to be a spy and were shot. Hence, it was a very risky business indeed.

It is hard to compare the life of a Prisoner of War in the UK with that of his counterpart in Germany, as I have little or no knowledge of how the Allies treated POWs daily. However, it is undoubtedly true to say that the Germans as captors were a mean lot in many ways. Some of their camp rules were miserable and served only to make life much harder than necessary. I could never see any justification for water rationing. The water supply was turned on for two periods per day, in the morning and evening, for washing and showering. Everyone was on a rota for a shower, and your time under the shower was limited precisely. This meant that when next in the queue, you stood as close as possible to the chap who was showering and caught every drop of water on your body. If you had some soap, you used the spray to start lathering up. If I remember rightly, the shower time was between thirty and forty seconds. There was always an "umpire" on duty, who had a watch and bellowed the changeover order at precisely the right time.

Dishwashing also had to be carried out during the "water on" period, and pots had to be filled ready for the evening meal, as well as intervening cups of tea. All were highly organised and ran to strict rotas. Each room had a similar rota for weekly cooks, dishwashers, room cleaners, etc.

Electricity was also rationed, and lights were out at 9:00 pm (10:00 pm camp time). Cooking, of course, depended entirely on whether there was anything to cook. The Germans provided little food, mainly consisting of boiled potatoes, thin, watery vegetable soup, and acorn coffee. On occasion, we received a loaf of bread. This was rather square in section, made of a very dark substance, and sprinkled on top with sawdust. All food was shared equally by the room's occupants, and each ate the same as the others. There was never any argument or cheating about this; at least, I never experienced any. The Kreigies had their sort of Orderly Room, which was positioned by the main gate and was again manned by a rota, and each Goon was logged as he entered or left the camp. If anyone was seriously ill, the matter was reported to the Orderly Room, which would then send a message to the Forelager. Hopefully, the Kreigie would get to see a Doctor, and I believe there was some hospital hut on the Forelager - although I never saw it.

There was a camp Dentist, a British man called Captain Hooper. He was captured at Dunkirk in 1940. His surgery was also in the forelager, a bare room containing a chair and a small cupboard. On top of it was his pathetic array of instruments, which included a dental drill. Here again, the miserable Germans would only allow him to work for one and a half hours per day, although he would, I am sure, have willingly given all his waking hours to the job. He was allowed into the main camp every afternoon ostensibly to watch whatever sports were in progress. He secreted a pair or two of forceps about his clothing and spent his time going from room to room, taking out teeth from those who were only too willing to get rid of troublesome teeth. As I arrived at Stalag Luft III in October 1943, I was again suffering from a toothache, and although it was bearable at first, it worsened after a month or so. I therefore put my name on the list to see the dentist. This was sometime in November, and my turn to see Captain Hooper came around in August 1944. There were no such things as aspirins, etc, so you can imagine how I felt after waiting nine months. I tried everything I could to loosen and perhaps remove the offending tooth, but to no avail.

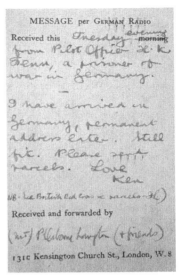

Message from Ken back home: "I have arrived in Germany. Still fit. Please send parcels. Love, Ken.

Imagine my delight when I got the message to be at the front gate to join the dentist's party. This was the system. There was a daily group of twenty-five patients who were marched under guard, of course, to the surgery. As I said, the dentist had ninety minutes to see twenty-five chaps, so I will leave you to work out that bit of arithmetic. We all sat on the floor around the room—a guard with us and another guard outside the door. At long, long, long last, I sat on the chair.

"Take them all out," I said, and I meant it!" Sorry—I don't have the time," he replied. "Where is the aching one?" I pointed to it, and he stuck in the drill and wound it round and round until he was sure that all decay had been removed. A filling was banged in. "Next!" he shouted.

I was in heaven to have gotten rid of the toothache, but I was very disappointed that I still had a mouthful of very poor teeth. However, now I was on the list. I managed six more visits, and each time, a tooth was drilled and filled. Luckily, I had no more toothache, but over the past months, I really had been close to despair, as you may well imagine. Having a toothache for a weekend was bad enough, but month after month, it was no joke. Captain Hooper did a sterling job while he was a Prisoner of War, and if any Serviceman deserved a medal, he did, and I hope that his efforts were recognised somewhere along the line. He persisted in his applications to the Germans for more and better equipment, but he was consistently disappointed. There is a rider to this episode, which I shall recount later.

"Circuit bashing" was a name given to walking around the perimeter of the compound, just inside the trip wire, and was indulged in by most Kreigies daily. It helped maintain a moderate level of fitness and was also helpful in discreet conversations when one could not be overheard. Hence, escape schemes and all matters concerning escape were discussed in this manner.

On one of these outings, I ran across my friend from 234 Squadron - Rover McLeod, the Canadian who had put me through my paces the first morning I joined the squadron. He had come to grief on an operation over France and had been forced to bail out. Therefore, we met on occasion and brought our experiences up to date. I also met several other pilots whom I had known on the squadrons. It seemed such a long time since the operational days, and yet it wasn't really, but so very much had happened since.

Winter had now set in, and I wondered - as everyone did - how many winters we would have to survive in this place.

Chapter 30

The Year of 1944

Christmas and New Year came and went, but left no impression. The most important thing was continued survival, both physically and mentally.

It was something of a danger to think too much of home, relations, and friends - not that I had many of the latter, but the comforts of home and family life are indisputable. I spent many an hour thinking of my long-lost father and wished he were still around so that I could get to know him. However, that was all in the imagination and was impossible to attain. The thought of a favourite meal was forever present, and it was around this time that I swore to myself that I would never again be cold or hungry - even if I had to steal to accomplish them. The Red Cross Food parcels arrived spasmodically, and it had been a rule of the camp to keep a couple of parcels per prisoner in stock in case of a real emergency. This meant, of course, about twenty-odd thousand, and in the end, it turned out to be a lifesaver. It occurred at some point that the Germans thought that escaping equipment of all sorts was being sent to us via the food parcels. Therefore, the next couple of issues were a bit of a nightmare.

A line of Goons was behind a long table, and a stack of Red Cross parcels behind them. When your time came, you arrived before a Goon carrying whatever receptacle you could lay your hands on. A large dish, a bucket, a basin, or whatever. The parcel was opened, and all the tins of food turned out. Remember that a food parcel was a means of survival and that each mouthful was precious and always savoured. Each tin was opened in turn and emptied, with a careful inspection of the contents, before being emptied into your container. Thus, you ended up with a mixture of powdered milk and condensed milk, sardines, bacon, hard Biscuits, margarine, prunes, etc. It was a sacrilege. Fortunately, they did not throw in the cigarettes. It was then a question of rushing back to your room and extracting what solid bits you could from the revolting mixture. There was only one thing that could be done with the rest. Heat it and eat it as a sort of semi-solid soup. But, as happens in many aspects of life, the Goons got fed up with the chore and slipped in the odd unopened tin after performing this operation a hundred times or so.

Not one piece of escaping aid was ever discovered, so after two issues in this manner, the whole project was disbanded. Thank God. It was an awful waste of essential sustenance, all of which reminds me of a room project.

We had seen a cat on occasions wandering about, and an idea was initiated. That was to catch the animal and use it as food. This scheme was discussed, and although the idea initially seemed repugnant, it could be said that it was just an animal, and had we been discussing a chicken, a duck, or a sheep, there would have been little problem. However, it was decided to put the plan into action, and a scheme was devised to draw lots in one way or another. Number One out of the hat would catch the animal. Number Two would kill it. Number Three would skin it, Numbers Four and Five would butcher it, and Number Six would find a means of cooking it. The scheme failed before the draw, as further discussions established that even if drawn to kill, no one in our room would actually go ahead and carry out the killing. Although we were all consistently hungry, we must not have reached the stage of starvation.

Reading formed an essential part of our routine, and here again, the faithful Red Cross had provided us with a library over the years. Some of the more seasoned prisoners and those of a more studious nature put themselves on a course of study. Digger Young, in our room, had acquired some medical books and even a skeleton (which appears in a photograph) from the Red Cross. Whether or not he continued his medical studies after the war, I do not know. The forever-present hunger and the winter cold were not conducive to settling down to study. However, people are different, and some cope with it better than others. In relation to the cold, some prisoners were better off than others in terms of clothing. I think I have mentioned before that I had very little clothing because I started my life as a prisoner in June in the Mediterranean. Fighter pilots accustomed to comparatively short operations tended to wear no flying clothing at all, except for flying boots, but again, these were practically nonexistent overseas in warm climates.

The Bomber Crews operating from the UK on six or eight-hour trips typically wore the leather flying jackets known as "Irvine" jackets over a full battle dress uniform, which was more fortunate. Heavy clothing in the cramped conditions of a Fighter tended to restrict movement. It was known that fighter pilots who decided to stay in bed, supposedly on dawn readiness, had only time to grab their flying boots when the Klaxon sounded and could be shot down wearing nothing but their pyjamas! A disaster no less.

Each room was given a meagre supply of compressed coal dust (briquettes), and these were saved up to occasionally have a gloriously warm room for a day. When this happened, it was remarkable how quickly the news spread, consequently bringing a large number of visitors to the room. It was during the winter of 1943/1944 or 1944/1945, I cannot remember which, that we, in our room, hatched a plot to combat this eternal winter cold.

When the compound cookhouse had sufficient ingredients to produce boiled potatoes or some watery soup, it had a supply of these briquettes to heat its stoves. We found the storeroom and decided to risk life and limb to obtain some. Armed guards with dogs patrolled the camp all night, and to get out of the window unseen and dash from the cover of one hut to another was, to say the least, rather hazardous. The principle of shooting first and asking questions later was always in force.

The three of us set off, and on arrival at the cookhouse hut, we lifted Mickey Rooney (the smallest member of our room) to squeeze through a small window. We then pushed three or four small sacks or such through to him. We left and returned half an hour later; he then returned the containers through the window, each loaded with briquettes. I think we did three or four trips on separate nights and then hid the fuel in every niche of our room that we could find. We had a beautiful, warm room for quite a time, and the consequent stream of visitors kept coming back and asking how we had succeeded in the fuel gathering. Their questions remained unanswered.

On occasion, the Goons would pounce upon a hut, and whether it was day or night, all the inmates would be ordered out. A meticulous search, mainly for tunnels and escape equipment, would then be conducted. During one of these searches, and to our utter dismay, as you can imagine, our coal supplies were found. We never repeated the exercise as they put bars across the fuel store window. It was excellent whilst it lasted, and was a great moral booster, but all good things come to an end.

The Ouija Board, used for forecasting the future and telling fortunes by those who believe in its powers, was in constant use by the members of one particular room. They wanted to know the answer to two questions only. Will we be able to get out of here safely, and what date will the war end? As you can imagine, all sorts of dates came in answer to their seances and were willingly publicised. Needless to say, none were accurate. I suppose it promoted the maintenance of sanity and was completely harmless.

Another item in constant production was solder. The many and varied tins from the Red Cross parcels are, of course, constructed mainly with the use of solder. A small blow lamp was made from a small tin, which was attached to a tapered pipe. A piece of string was submerged in the base container containing melted margarine. Again, a blowpipe was attached, which pointed into the flame. It was incredible to see how much heat could be produced by blowing down the tube into the flame. Certainly sufficient to melt solder. In this way, many things were constructed. One could either make one's own tool - say, a distillery - or hire one from someone else for a payment of cigarettes. These were used to distil alcohol produced from items like sultanas and sugar. This exercise was not undertaken very often as it entailed saving up one's meagre rations of the necessary ingredients. However, the Christmas of 1944/45 was notable for the alcohol available. The guards were somehow cajoled into partaking, and the place was in an uproar. Kreigies were being sick all over the place - neat alcohol is not an attractive drink - but it did serve its purpose at the time. I saw a hilarious theatre performance due to the actors' partaking in the stuff. The few Goons who succumbed to this pleasure were removed from their posts and never seen again. It was presumed that they ended up on the Russian Front for punishment.

There was a glorious sports day in 1944, and a grand parade led by the band, who played a particular piece of marching music, which annoyed the Goons, who rushed in and confiscated the instruments for a couple of weeks. There were several sideshows, too - one of which I remember was the Fire Dance. This turned out to be a fire of newspapers in a shallow trench, and at the appointed time, a Kriegie stepped into the trench to stamp out the fire. He used one leg only - and this leg was, in fact, a wooden one! Hilarious indeed and caused great laughter - all customers, of course, were sworn to secrecy before leaving.

Several escape projects were underway in 1943, but gained notoriety post-war in the form of a book and subsequently a film. The "Horse" referred to a vaulting horse, which, when carried out in the grounds and deposited on an exact spot, contained two Kreigies and their tools for tunnel digging. There were also three massive projects running simultaneously. These were three tunnels named Tom, Dick and Harry. The Ferrets found two, but the third was successful. Unfortunately, the outlet was slightly misjudged and came out short of the woods. However, the idea was to send out up to two hundred men each night until it was found. Unfortunately, after many months of intensive effort, the exit was discovered on the first night, but not until sixty or seventy Kreigiers had managed to escape.

The German hierarchy was informed of the success of this escape and caused great concern indeed, and the dreadful result was that forty-seven of the escapees ended up at Gestapo headquarters and were shot. This was awful, and everyone was stunned. Ian Cross, who was in our room, was one of the very unfortunate chaps. A memorial was built in their honour. The "Great Escape," as it was called, also formed the basis of a book and a film in later years. I did hear that only one Kreigie got to neutral Spain, but I could not vouch for the truth of this.

Ken on the bottom bunk; Ian Cross top right bunk. Flt Lt Cross was later executed on Hitler's orders after escaping in the Great Escape.

Food, of course, was still scarce, but on occasions, there was an issue of acorn coffee and also black bread. A large loaf of this dense stuff would produce about forty pieces with very careful slicing. Red Cross packets of seed were very hard to grow in the extremely sandy soil, but they provided me with my first introduction to corn on the cob - an item I have revelled in ever since. One hut housed a communal toilet, a large brick-built pit with long pine logs along both sides. One had to balance precariously to get one's rear part on the far side of the log. Back to basics again!

We were sometimes visited by a couple of members of the Gestapo who would demand a roll call. During this, they would walk slowly along the files of Kreigie, searching each face in turn. This was, to say the least, petrifying, and the odd fellow was taken off, never to be seen again. You talk about wishing the ground would open up and swallow you—well, now you know how we all felt.

Home and family were constantly on my mind, and I was forever wondering if I would ever see them again. Postcards to write home were occasionally issued and, of course, were all censored, as were the letters from home. I don't know how many letters were sent to me, but I do know that I didn't receive many of them. Some lads occasionally received "Dear John" letters, which could have disastrous effects. If the reader is unfamiliar with a "Dear John" letter, I will explain that it was typically written by a wife, fiancée, or girlfriend who informed the recipient that they had begun alternative relationships for whatever reason. Some recipients could understand the reasons, but it was still a very unkind thing to do. Hate letters were also in existence, and I received one of these from a surprising source, who thought it was not right that I should be languishing in a prison camp whilst other men were fighting for their country! It was disturbing, to say the least, but I eventually attributed it to the sender's arrogance and ignorance.

The West Compound, which housed American aircrew, also contained band instruments. One day, they assembled on their side of the wire to give us a concert. They struck up a very popular Glenn Miller-type music, and hundreds of Kreigies assembled on our side to delight in the concert. The Goons in the watchtower didn't like it and opened fire with a machine gun. You have never seen a crowd disappear so fast. Luckily, no one was hurt, but it was typical of them to spoil what would have been a very entertaining interlude. I often thought it was a great pity that Officers were not allowed to work. This would have alleviated boredom and would no doubt have provided an opportunity to participate in subversive sabotage, as happened countless times when other ranks worked in factories, on the roads, and on the railways.

I met a Yorkshire navigator - and this, of course, is no reflection on that county - he had talked himself into believing that this life as a prisoner was preferable to being on bombing raids, which, like all operations, generally frightened the participant to death. He was, therefore, reasonably content with his lifestyle. I don't suppose he pursued this line of thought once he got back to the UK, which he did, and I met him in Blackpool years later when he was a shop manager.

I will end this chapter in 1944 with the outstanding news of that year. I cannot possibly explain the absolute delight when we heard the news of the Second Front. This was the Normandy invasion in June 1944. This was the biggest morale booster of all time. We received regular news bulletins from the secret radios, which were taken down by a half dozen Kreigies, who then set off around the huts and relayed the news items. I created a map of Northern France and continually updated my line as the Allies advanced. It was tremendous news and formed the basis of most conversations. The bombing of German cities, especially Berlin, was terrific news, and although one thought about the poor civilians, it was no doubt the means to an end. After all, it was a case of every man for himself, and they started the war anyway.

The question now in our minds was, can we manage to survive the rest of the war? It would be terrible to get so far and then, for some reason, fail to return to the UK.

Life henceforth took on a slightly different outlook.

Ken Cam

THIS PAGE IS DEDICATED TO KEN'S
STALAG LUFT III ROOMMATE,
FLT LT IAN CROSS,
WHO WAS SADLY EXECUTED ON
HITLER'S ORDERS

Chapter 31

On the Move Again

The winter of 1944/45 seemed to be colder than ever. We still donned all the clothing we possessed before getting into bed, and I kept up my walking exercise as much as possible. By now, the Russians were advancing from the East and the Allies from the West. We understood the Russians had reached the River Oder some thirty or forty miles from us. Rumours were rife, but we listened intently when the Kreigie came to the hut with the latest bulletins. All this time, it looked quite possible that the Russians might liberate us, and our future seemed to be very precarious indeed.

We knew of the German habit of springing surprises only too well - and these surprises never seemed to go in our favour. No reasons were ever given for these surprises, and we were left in the dark. The news items concerning the Allied advances were uplifting, but as always, we never knew our positions regarding movement or possible liberation. Never in our wildest dreams did we expect the surprise that was announced to us in early January 1945. An immediate appell was announced over the speakers. Everyone quickly paraded, and the Senior British Officer addressed us. We could not believe our ears. We were moving out - all twelve thousand of us - and had twenty-four hours to prepare ourselves. We were advised to prepare our personal belongings and chattels for departure. Food and clothing - nothing else mattered. Do not try to carry too much - essentials only.

To this end, the Red Cross parcel store was thrown open to everyone to help themselves. As I have said, each food parcel weighed about ten pounds, so one could not take many. We all had a couple of jolly good meals and prepared ourselves. Cigarettes were comparatively light to carry, and we had an excellent supply in our room. Bob Coste came from a wealthy Canadian family, all of whom had sent him loads of sweet Caporal cigarettes for months, working on the assumption that if only ten per cent reached him, then there would be plenty. It was a rule of our room that all of us were to help ourselves, which we did, but there was still more we could carry, so open house was declared, and as you may imagine, they soon disappeared. An awful lot of publicity is given these days to the disastrous effects of smoking, but they did provide solace and also abate hunger, so they had their undoubted benefits. I feverishly set about my preparation, as did everyone else, and I assembled what I thought was as adequate a load as I could manage.

The snow was thick on the ground, and it was bitterly cold. My big problem was footwear, and I wondered how long I could manage before having to walk barefoot. I then made myself a sort of sledge. I used the back legs of a chair, and from that base, I fabricated my sledge, which I loaded with what I thought would be light enough to pull and obviate the sledge's collapse. The next day, I was ready. I don't think anyone got a wink of sleep that night, and we spent our time planning our trek—a trek to where and for how long - nobody knew. We were assembled in columns of five abreast, with the armed guards walking along each side about twenty yards apart. And so our life in Stalag Luft III came to an end.

We were all aircrew and, as such, probably fitter than most forces members. However, people vary in their physical condition and mental ability to survive such arduous conditions. It is not a matter of boasting to say that you got through it—some do, and some don't.

Later, we understood that out of twelve hundred in our North Compound, some two hundred fell by the wayside—literally. The poor souls had just had enough and lay down in the snow and died. One could not really help them when they got to that stage. It was not as though anyone could carry a friend. The strength to do that was most certainly not available. I have wondered many times since how I would have got through torture, as some unfortunate people experienced. I concluded that I would have given up quite quickly, but then again, one doesn't know.

Don't ask me how many days and nights this first trek lasted—I have no idea—the whole thing seemed to be an endless nightmare. Occasionally, the seemingly infinite column was halted for a rest, and one just sat down where one could.

Many years later, within the last five years, Betty and I were on a coach holiday to Southsea, near Portsmouth. One evening, we got a taxi and asked the driver to take us to an old pub in the docks area. Sitting at the end of the bar in the pub was an obvious regular, and as he was of rather a voluble nature, he struck up a conversation. He had been in the Air Force, but he was not involved in operations. The conversation revealed that I had been aircrew and had spent a couple of years as a POW, ending up in Stalag Luft III. "Don't tell me you were on the Death March? He questioned. I explained where I had been, but I had never heard it referred to as that before. Without further ado, he shook my hand and bought me a pint. He said another pub regular was on the same "Death March" - and perhaps he would be in later on. But I never met him; back to the story.

I know little of our route, but I do remember passing through a small town called Darmstadt, and I think that it was in this place that a surprising thing happened. We soon discovered that we were being halted for the night, and a hundred or so of us were shepherded towards a building. We were ordered to go inside, and what met our eyes was a miracle. We were in a glass factory, and the ovens were still hot. The warmth was an absolute luxury, and we bedded down on the floor. I still had with me a small tin of boiled bacon, which was occasionally to be found in a British Red Cross parcel. I placed it in the large oven and guarded it zealously until it was hot. What an unbelievable treat! I shall never forget it. That night, we all got a good sleep. On an ensuing night, another strange thing happened. We were back on the march, and may I say that by this time, our German guards had begun to fail in their duties. They were all appreciably older than us and, believe it or not, could not take the conditions as well as we, who had survived so far.

There was no point in attempting an escape in these wintry conditions. Common sense told us to stay with the column in the hope of better things to come. However, there was a sudden and quick thaw on this night or evening back on the march. This brought mixed blessings. Seeing the back of the bitter cold was fabulous, but my sledge soon became a burden. I was dragging it along the roads from which the snow had melted. I persisted in doing so and resolved to alter my mode of transport at the first available daylight opportunity. This I did during the first halt the next morning. But that night lives in my memory as complete and utter drudgery, which seemed interminable. I unloaded my dwindling possessions, keeping the blanket and the remaining food, and then kicked the faithful sledge into the roadside. It had served me well, but all things come to an end. The German Officers in charge of the whole procedure rode up and down on motorcycles and sidecars, and no doubt availed themselves of long and peaceful rests in comfort. Of course they did!

But that night of the thaw was probably the worst night of the whole march, and although I say so myself, it was nothing but a dogged determination to come through it that kept me going. The next morning, after the super warm sojourn in the glass factory, a comparatively good sleep, and some food, we were in a much better frame of mind and sort of ready to face the oncoming day.

For some reason best known to the Goons, the American contingent had been separated and headed off in a different direction. Years later, I heard that they ended up in Moosburg, but I am not sure. After this ordeal, and the war itself was over, a certain mentality was required to research the whole episode in one's life. I had no such desire then, so now I write only what I can remember, which I suppose is a memoir in the true sense of the word.

During the march, which was more correctly termed a walk, one's immediate companion was constantly changing. Some dropped back, and others came forward, but there was little conversation. I had lost considerable weight in the prison camp, but now I was, as you may well imagine, getting rather thin. There were still dropouts - goodness knows what happened to them.

There was a surprising end to this first phase of the journey from Stalag Luft III. Please don't ask me how far we had come or how long it had taken us. I do not have the faintest idea, but we entered a small town and were surprised to find ourselves halted on the way to a railway station. "Oh my, not again," I thought. "Not those dreadful cattle trucks."

As on every other occasion when the column halted, we sat down in the road on whatever baggage we had and waited for the next move. I sat and pondered the present situation. Surely, life in a cattle truck was preferable to continually being on one's feet; at least it would be warmer, and one would be able to rest. And so, in a way, it was somewhat of a pleasure to climb into the truck once more.

Yet the unanswered question remained: How long would we be in the trucks, and what was our destination? We thought the journey was merely to keep us away from the advancing Allied forces. The train started and, as before, frequently stopped. The train journey finally came to an end, and we set off once again on a walk. It was daylight, and we found ourselves approaching the familiar sight of yet another prison camp.

This was a camp called Marlag Und Milag Nord, designed to accommodate captured naval personnel and situated outside Bremen. We had travelled one way or the other from Sagan, south of Berlin, to the north-west of Germany. This was a much smaller camp, and we settled in. Red Cross parcels were again in circulation—a lifesaver—and we rested and ate as much as possible. I should imagine we were now into March 1945. But what of the future? What would be sprung upon us next?

Chapter 32

Rest and be Thankful

The weather had greatly improved, and the news from the battlefronts was good. The end of the war seemed to be in sight, so all we had to do was sit and wait and ensure that we were still alive when liberation came. But it wasn't quite as easy as that. It was probably around ten days later that the news came as a sudden surprise, again. We had two days' notice to prepare ourselves to move out this time. Would this dreadful war never end?

I immediately set to work and gathered together articles to make, if possible, a small truck. I hurriedly looked around all corners of the camp and eventually got hold of a small tea chest and some wood, and I was amazed to find an old mangle. From this, I took a wheel and a shaft and persisted in searching for another wheel. I was delighted to find another wheel - not the same diameter, but who cared? I made my lopsided two-wheeled truck. It had sufficient room in the tea chest to house the baggage of two, so I recruited another Kreigie to join me, and we agreed to pull the thing on alternate days. Wonderful! I felt I could now tackle whatever lay ahead.

The short rest was over, and I was thankful for my well-being. My new companion was an Air Gunner, and although we were constantly together day and night for the next couple of months, I cannot remember his name or where he came from. Such is life and forgetfulness, but we saw each other through the next phase.

At the appointed time, the column once again set off. The daylight hours were lengthening, and as we approached spring, the weather was appreciably milder, although there was a fair amount of rain. The routine was simple. We walked from dawn to dusk with occasional halts, but as darkness approached, we stopped, and that was where you spent the night. Generally, the guards were becoming lax and were occasionally replaced. On one occasion, the guard alongside our particular section of the column disappeared and was replaced by a typical young blue-eyed blond chap who had been a fighter pilot in the Luftwaffe. He had been shot down and had injured one of his legs. He was an autocratic, self-opinionated man who looked upon us as the scum of the earth and carried his rifle always at the ready and gave the impression that he was willing to shoot anyone to whom he took a dislike. I kept as far out of his sight as I could. But it didn't take long in the circumstances for him to realise that his injuries were causing him trouble, and in a matter of days, he came down off his high horse and became somewhat friendly, as did the vast majority of the guards. Although they were regularly fed, they seemed to suffer more than the prisoners.

Discipline slackened considerably, and there were many instances where a prisoner would help a guard by carrying his rifle for him! Unbelievable, but true. Sometimes, we would halt for half a day or so, and on those occasions, the prisoners would take every opportunity to steal items and food from the fields and farmyards. Odd cabbage and potatoes were acquired in this way, especially as on most nights, we were ordered to spend the night in the fields. Surprisingly, on one occasion, a pig was stolen, killed, and butchered in no time at all. Again, one day, a farm cart was pinched and pulled along by a bunch of prisoners who willingly put their kit on the cart and joined the merry band in the pulling. The nearby guards also put their packs and rifles on the cart! It was turning into a Fred Karno's Circus. But as usual, the delights ended, and we soon returned to normal.

My companion and I each had a blanket; we slept back to back and head to toe, sharing the two blankets. It was miserable when it rained at night, but we survived. The route took us through Hamburg. Now, Hamburg had suffered many a bombing raid, and as we walked through the place, the population made no bones about their hatred of us. It must have gladdened their hearts to see a never-ending column of dirty, dishevelled British and Allied aircrew walking slowly past them. Shouting, spitting, and throwing things became a regular feature of our progress through the city.

We passed through Hamburg and were still heading east until we eventually reached the outskirts of Lübeck, on the Baltic Sea. Here, we were halted for what turned out to be the last time, and our particular section - I suppose two or three hundred - were to take up "residence" on a large farm estate. Here again, I was lucky and got a space on the upper floor of a large barn. The luxury of sleeping on dry hay will be obvious. Eventually, everything was dried out, and we were much more comfortable. Life dragged slowly by until the end of April, when news came that the end of the war was imminent. Spirits soared, and life became much more bearable. I was able to clean myself up to a large extent, but washing clothing was a problem. I cannot remember the food situation while living on the farm estate. The guards, if indeed you could describe them as such, had given up and were trying to make friends with us—how things had changed! We had been on the move for a long time, and since we left Stalag Luft III, an incredible four months had passed! Apart from odd periods such as cattle truck journeys, a short period in Marlag Und Milag Nord, and odd occasions when we had spent a night in the glass factory, and later in a barn, we had been outside day and night. The nights were generally pretty miserable, especially when it rained, and I often recalled my grandma saying that I must not wear damp clothing or sit or lie on wet ground. Good advice, no doubt, but I do not seem to have suffered in the least.

In the barn at our final stopping place, I recall feeling a movement across my face and head on the first night or two, but I attributed it to odd spiders or similar creatures. However, being so desperately tired and weary, I disregarded them. Eventually, I realised that my head was on a rat run, so I moved so that my feet were where my head had been, and the matter was solved.

The war news filtered through and continued to improve. We were accustomed to rumours circulating, so everything was treated with a certain amount of suspicion. Nevertheless, I began to make plans, and thoughts of home and family became even more prevalent and exciting.

How were they all at home? What exactly had happened over the last two years? Again, I longed to talk to my father on my return, and it seemed that as the last few years passed, I had missed him more and more. This did not, of course, detract from the love I had for my mother, grandmother, and sister, but being able to talk to a man was something different. Still, that could never be, and I had to get used to it. We were a small family, and I longed to see them all. I was still a long way from home and resolved that I should take no chances and not do anything stupid. I was rested, excited, and raring to go.

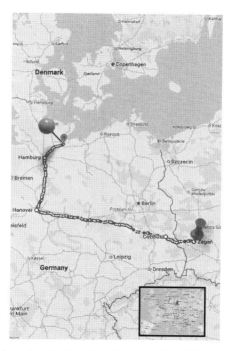

Forced march to freedom. To the best of our knowledge, this is the route that Ken took between January 1945 and May 1945.

Chapter 33

Liberation

You all know what the word liberation means - or do you? There is a liberation of thought, a liberation of words, morals, deeds, and behaviour. Then, there is liberation from a captor who had complete control of your life and well-being. Looking back over the last two years, we had not fared as badly as others. I have a Dutch friend who, at the age of nineteen, had been captured by the Germans in Amsterdam whilst working for the intensive underground movement in Holland. He was immediately taken out of Holland and spent four years in the renowned concentration camp at Buchenwald - and he survived it! Since the war and his return to his native country, he has dedicated most of his spare time to travelling around his country and lecturing to all who would listen, from schoolchildren to older people. The theme of all his talks was "The Bastard Germans". And who would blame him?

So liberation came in the form of a spearhead of advancing troops from the Cheshire Regiment. We all surged around our visitors, and an Army Captain stood on his vehicle and informed us that he would immediately notify his headquarters and guaranteed that he would organise transport and have us all out within forty-eight hours.

As part of the leading scout car of our liberators was another man called Frank Wright, and I learned about this twenty-odd years later when I met him. This is the coincidence I mentioned in Chapter 16. It turned out that Frank Wright was present at the docks at the Port of Bône in North Africa and saw the lone Spitfire, which I was flying. He saw me chasing the Italian Fighter Bomber, which succeeded in dropping a bomb right on the Royal Navy Ship "Ajax". Frank Wright was not only one of my liberators; he had seen me attempt to stop the Italian bomber, and he remembered the incident well.

After 48 hours, there was no sign of the lorries the Army Captain had promised, and I decided to take matters into my own hands. In retrospect, this was somewhat foolish—just what I said I would not do. A front line of advancing troops is a rather fluid thing - very changeable. One day, any particular territory could be in Allied hands, and the next day, it could be back under the control of the Germans. However, this did not occur to me at the time. I had little or no belongings beyond the clothes I stood up in. At this time, I had a pair of American khaki trousers, a dirty white sweatshirt, and an enormous pair of boots, all of which I had acquired by various means. There was certainly no means of identification except for the dog tag around my neck, which showed my POW Number. Nevertheless, I was determined, and I set off to walk. Westward was all I thought of. Being dressed as I was, it was indeed quite possible that any soldier of either side could shoot me without question. Front-line troops, whoever they were, were trigger-happy and would shoot first and ask questions later. But good fortune was with me as I walked along a country lane. I suppose I had travelled about five miles when I saw a jeep-like vehicle approaching. What should I do? I decided to keep on walking, hoping that whoever it was would ignore me. Not so. The German amphibious jeep-type vehicle stopped. Its occupants were a German officer and a German driver. These were front-line soldiers, and they were armed. They had no idea who I was. I suppose I looked more like a peasant than anyone else. I was scared and awaited the next move. What happened was absolutely amazing. It remains so vivid in my memory to this day.

They both got out of the jeep and approached me. The officer, believe it or not, saluted me. Although British Forces never salute unless they wear headgear, I returned the salute. Surely, I thought, they are not surrendering. But they were. I pointed to their revolvers and made a motion for them to hand them over to me. They complied.

I put the guns on the vehicle's front seat, turned to them and said:

"British Kriegerfarganer", and pointed to the way I had come. Off they went on foot. I can only presume that they, like many others, were glad to be out of the war. I got into the jeep, turned it around, and continued on my way with a light heart. An amazing story - I'm sure you'll agree.

I pressed on with my journey, hoping against hope that no one would take a potshot at me and my German vehicle. I supposed that I was a target for either side, being out of uniform. But, once more, my good luck held. Looking at the maps now, my motoring episode didn't last very long, but at the time, it seemed a long way to me! I arrived at Luneburg, where I saw a large barracks that the British had already occupied. I drove through the entrance gates and found the guardroom. I told them who I was and asked for a bed for the night. This was immediately granted, and I parked the jeep. I was weary again, and after a meal, I took to my bed and slept through until the next morning.

On waking, I thought I would ask for some breakfast and then continue my journey westward. Things were going fine. Or were they? I must mention here that my stomach had shrunk considerably, so I could only eat small amounts of food. This state of affairs persisted for some considerable time after liberation and my eventual return to the UK.

I emerged from the building to get into my vehicle. What vehicle? Someone had swiped it! I returned immediately to the guardroom to report the incident. It was all to no avail; it had gone. An officer in the guardroom informed me that a troop train from the local station ran through to Brussels. That's for me, I thought, and asked for directions to the station. I arrived just too late. The train had left. I found out later that the train was involved in a head-on collision with another train, and upwards of a hundred Army Personnel were killed!

I left the station, found the right road out of town, and started thumbing a lift. Eventually, a small truck stopped. Aboard were two British Army lads who asked where I was going. "Brussels, "I said. "Jump in," they replied, "That's where we are going." They took me all the way. More good luck! I told them immediately that I was a liberated Prisoner of War. They were quite sympathetic. I do not know what job they were doing, but they seemed to know quite a lot about what was going on. They told me that they knew of two places in Brussels that were quite close to each other and would no doubt be of interest to me. They were the RAF Officers' Club and a Reception Centre set up in a hotel for escaped and liberated prisoners of war. I elected to be taken to the RAF Club, which they did, but first showed me where the POW Reception Centre was. Can you imagine my good fortune in meeting these two?

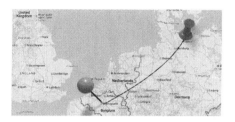

Ken's journey from Lübeck to Brussels

I entered the portals of what seemed to be a rather magnificent baronial place and was questioned by an Airman who sat at a desk in the entrance hall. I explained who I was, and he seemed to believe me without question. "The bar and restaurant are upstairs," he said. So up I went. I was still dressed like something the dog had brought in, but I didn't care. I entered the large room, stopped for a moment, and looked around. There was a large array of Officers in their best blue uniforms, accompanied by their ladies.

It has been said often, probably as a matter of statistical fact, that only about ten or fifteen per cent of any of the three Services ever experience being involved in battles of whatever sort there may be —on land, at sea, or in the air. As I looked around, the thought that went through my mind was that these characters were some of the other 85 or 90%. The luck of the draw, I suppose - like a chap I met in Blackpool many years later who had been an Army Captain and had spent the entire war in Grange-over-Sands, and Windermere! Sour grapes, perhaps!

Back to the immediate surroundings. I went up to the bar and told the corporal barman who I was. He repeated this to an officer a little way down the bar, who immediately came and shook my hand. Give the officer a gin and tonic, he said to the barman. I had never had a gin and tonic before, and it tasted delicious. Before I knew where I was, there were half a dozen lined up on the bar awaiting my attention. Various Officers came across and asked what had happened to me and where I had been. During these conversations, a plate of sandwiches appeared, along with a packet of cigarettes and a box of matches. I was complete, and I sampled all that was available, probably rather greedily, but why not? Life - at the moment- was outstandingly good. Bear in mind, though, that I had partaken of alcohol but twice in my life before this day. Once was the bottle of cheap local Algerian wine on Christmas Eve in 1942, and the other time was partaking of what was ostensibly a raisin liqueur - brewed in Stalag Luft III- again at Christmas time, but in 1944.

This then explains why—long before I had finished the six gin and tonics, I quietly sank into an armchair and slid out of consciousness. What more could I have wished for? My new friends politely left me to dream my dreams, and I awoke in the early hours of the morning. The barman had been instructed to stay with me until I came round, which he did and led me to a bedroom, where I again lapsed into slumber.

The next time I woke up, there was plenty of activity in the Club, and I found an officer who looked to be a permanent member of the Club Staff. I thanked him and his colleagues for their hospitality and said that I thought I had better go and find the POW Reception Centre, hopefully get cleaned up, and organise some clean clothing. The officer thought that was a good idea and said I should be most welcome when I returned. I again thanked him and left.

I soon found the Reception Centre, which had been pointed out to me by the two Army lads who brought me to Brussels. I went in and was greeted and sincerely welcomed by an Army officer at a desk in the entrance hall. He told me that there were no formalities, except to give my Number, Rank, and Name. He then took me to a room where I was given underclothing and an Army battle dress, blouse, trousers, socks, and boots. He showed me to the bathroom and bedroom, which he said were at my disposal for as long as I wished. The dining room, he said, was open for light meals twenty-four hours a day. Each morning, he told me, a truck would arrive at about 8:30 am to take any arrivals out to the airfield to be flown home to the UK.

What service, indeed! But did I want it? I had a lovely, long bath and a shave, then got dressed and headed down to the dining room. I had a light snack and went out to look around the streets.

Liberation and freedom! I was on top of the world, and what is more, I did not want to come off the top of the world—not yet, anyway. I returned to the RAF Club and was warmly greeted again. It was now early evening, and I was offered some food. I knew I couldn't eat a lot, so I gladly accepted a sandwich. The drinks were again free, and I had a twinge of conscience about having no money, but I didn't let it bother me a lot. Surely I had paid in advance for whatever came my way. I enjoyed chatting and found myself on the dance floor with a female. I couldn't say any more about her than that. I do not know who she was, nor did I care. It was all very pleasant. During one of these dances, I saw a fellow I vaguely recognised. He was somewhat dishevelled, and I spoke to him. It was another Kreigie. "Stalag Luft III ?" I asked. "Yes," he said, "I've just arrived." I told him that I had arrived a couple of days before - how many days it was exactly, I could not say, and it flashed through my mind that I was no longer to be the "talk of the town". I had lost my advantage and wondered how long it would be before the place was swarming with lads from Stalag Luft III.

Later that evening, I returned to the reception hotel and went to bed. The next morning, I was up, washed, shaved, breakfasted, and out of the place before the lorry came. I expect that they knew what I was doing, but they didn't bother me. I had another enjoyable day and once again ended up at the Club. The hospitality didn't seem to be diminishing at all, but I resolved that the next morning, I would be ready for the 8:30 truck. I had enjoyed my time in Brussels, but was keen to be on the move again, which must have been after a four or five-day stay there. It was a good exercise in rehabilitation —a process that lasted longer than I expected. These days, they call the condition "post-traumatic stress disorder "and make a big fuss about it, but in 1945, to get rehabilitated was entirely up to yourself - to get on with it, so to speak. The 8:30 am truck arrived on time, and I climbed aboard.

Chapter 34

Homeward Bound

I suppose that there were about half a dozen of us on the truck. We were all dressed alike with our uniforms issued at the reception hotel, but it appeared that I was the only RAF member there. The others were Army lads from various POW camps. We arrived at an airfield, and there, sitting on the tarmac with its engines running, was a Lancaster Bomber. A member of the crew checked us off a list of names, and I was shown to the nose of the aircraft, where I lay to watch the takeoff. Quite interesting, as it was significantly slower than a Spitfire. So I lay in the nose and watched the countryside go past, and my thoughts were of Great Britain, of England, and home. Again, I wished I could go home to talk to Dad.

We were crossing the English Channel when a crew member brought me a copy of a magazine called "Picture Post". This no longer exists, but was a periodical that I believe was published fortnightly, consisting entirely of pictures with explanatory legends. No articles at all, as I remember. He opened the magazine to a page and remarked that he was sure that I would find the pictures of great interest. And so I did. Very much so. There was a series of photos showing returning POWs being enthusiastically greeted by attractive young nurses from the Red Cross. How I longed for the loving embrace of a woman! In fact, if the truth were known, I longed for a great many things! I devoured the contents of the Picture Post and lay there watching and dreaming.

We crossed the South Coast of England, and everything looked so very peaceful. My mind was at peace. For the millionth time, I thanked my God that I was still in one piece and back in the UK. Unfortunately, a temporary disappointment was around the corner. We landed at RAF Cosford, which is halfway between Telford in Shropshire and Wolverhampton. I climbed down from the aircraft and excitedly walked towards the reception ladies. As I approached, my enthusiasm died somewhat as I was greeted by a Red Cross Nurse who must have been well into her sixties. She offered her hand and said, "Welcome home, young man. Please follow me." So much for my Picture Post welcome!

Ken's last leg of the journey back to the UK

She questioned me about my health as we walked towards a large aircraft hangar. What followed was very surprising. I had never known such an organisation before in the RAF. A great deal of thought and preparation had gone into the returning POW Reception Centre. It was unbelievably slick. The nurse took me to a desk in the hangar and then left. I was asked the usual questions: Number, Rank, and Name. Next was a series of medical examinations, each one specialising in a different part of the body. The final one was a dentist who, after his examination, said, "You have had teeth filled in Germany." Yes, I answered, "I have seven fillings."

The fillings contained poisonous elements, and the teeth had to be removed immediately. He gave me a time to return in the afternoon.

The next stage in the proceedings was a long table with about half a dozen Women's Auxiliary Air Force personnel, all with sewing equipment, and backed by shelves of RAF uniforms and clothing. They checked your Name, Rank, and Number on a list and produced a full kit of clothes. All the Army lads had gone off elsewhere, so there were only a dozen Air Force chaps going through the procedure. I tried on the trousers, blouse, and forage cap, and any necessary alterations were made immediately. I took the underclothes and, as instructed, went to have a shower and change my Army clothing for the RAF kit. I returned to the tailoring table. Everything had been completed, and my Flight Lieutenant Rank Stripes, my Pilot Wings, and my Medal Ribbons were already in place. What a wonderful system!

I handed in the Army kit and had my photograph taken. The final stage was an interview by MI5, the Secret Service lot, who mainly wanted to know where I had been and whether I could give them names of any Germans who were responsible for atrocities of any sort.

The interview was completed, and I was directed to the Officers' Mess, where I was allocated a room and informed that the dining hall was open throughout the day and night, allowing me to eat at my convenience. The meals, again, were of the light snack variety, which, as they knew, was all we could cope with. The entire reception procedure took a remarkably short period, unlike the usual run of things, which typically involved a lot of waiting time.

I reported back to the dentist, who conducted a thorough examination and determined that the situation was not as severe as initially thought. I cannot remember whether he said that I would have to lose four teeth and that he could save three, or the other way around. He extracted the requisite number and asked me to see him the next day. It was all so different from the Stalag Luft III dentist Captain Hooper, who, if you remember, had worked under such difficult conditions.

The rest of the day passed amiably enough, and the following morning, I was given an Identity Card, complete with a photograph, a Pay Book, some cash, a Ration Book, and a Travel Warrant to any destination in the UK that I specified. Telephone calls were free and un-rationed. All that remained was my second trip to the dentist and a brief interview to determine whether I had any problems that they could assist me with. I was given a month's leave and had to decide which job I would like to do until my demobilisation was due. I could opt for Administration, Stores and Equipment Officer, Flying Control, or Mechanical Transport Officer. Thinking of the possible source of petrol, which, of course, was still severely rationed, I chose the latter. I would receive my posting at a later date.

After the dentist, I drew my railway warrant and was informed that every train in the country would have a few compartments to be used only by returning POWs. Another stroke of genius. It was very accurate that one had little or no conversation for civilians - one felt very much withdrawn and a stranger in their company. A booklet of advice on how to deal with an ex-prisoner and what sort of behaviour to expect from him was sent to my home. This booklet included advice pertaining to small but frequent meals, a lack of conversation, and an urge to move on somewhere else every few days. These things were all true.

I sent a message home via a friend's telephone, stating which Blackpool station I would arrive at and at what time. I set off on my final part of the journey.

Chapter 35

Home at Last

The train arrived at Blackpool Central Station, and as I walked down the platform, I spotted my mother waiting in a small crowd of people at the barrier. We are not a demonstrative family, and although sincere, the reunion was true to form. My mother, of course, was very concerned about my physical well-being, which, apart from having lost a considerable amount of weight, was alright. I was quite fit, really, and my problems, if you can call them that, were in the mind. It perhaps seems peculiar to the reader, and it is no doubt an awful admission, but I remember very few details of my arrival at home and seeing the rest of our small family. My mind was bulging with the knowledge that, at long last, I was, in fact, home, but I cannot recall conversations at all. Strange but true.

The homestead had not changed. I had been away for a period approaching three years. My embarkation leave before the journey to Algiers was in September 1942. My Sister, Kathleen, had got married in 1944, having decided quite rightly that it was pointless to wait until the end of the war, which, of course, was anyone's guess. It may be interesting to note here that, due to severe rationing, meals in restaurants, albeit of a very basic nature, were limited to a cost of five shillings per head (25p), and such gatherings as wedding receptions were also limited to twenty guests. The whole reception, therefore, cost the princely sum of Five Pounds! Sydney had joined the household and was indeed a very welcome addition.

The booklet about returning prisoners of war had explained that I would be restless and eager to depart for other places until I had mentally settled down. This proved to be correct, and every few days I had to be off to somewhere or other. I must have given the family great concern, but I had no option.

My friend Douglas was, of course, still flying with the RAF and, after a serious flying accident in Normandy, had lengthy treatment for his spinal injury. However, he was at this time instructing at a Service Flying Training School at Millfield, up near Berwick on Tweed. I managed to visit him, and it was an excellent reunion. He was able to obtain permission for me to join him in an American Harvard training aircraft, and I shall never forget the utter delight I experienced in getting to the controls once again. Unfortunately, after two days, I had the uncontrollable urge to be on the move again. The month's leave went by all too quickly, and my posting came through. I was ordered to report to RAF Tilstock as Mechanical Transport Officer. Tilstock is located in Shropshire, just south of Whitchurch. There was a certain amount of flying there, but I cannot remember what sort. In any case, I had no part in it. I assumed my duties and was joined by a long-serving Flight Sergeant, a few other Sergeants and Corporals, and approximately a dozen drivers. It was, after my previous responsibilities in the RAF, rather mundane and somewhat dull, but life in the Officers' Mess was good. I suppose that I must have done a reasonable job, as I was posted to a much larger station after some time. This was RAF Crossby-on-Eden, located near the town of Longton, north of Carlisle. It was the same sort of job - but more of it.

But, before my leave at home had finished, and as the next chapter is somewhat concerned with rehabilitation, I shall interrupt the narrative by recording an incident which I found to be amusing at the time. However, I can imagine that those present who had not been in the Services did not agree with my opinion. I was invited to attend a small ceremony at my pre-war place of work, the Fylde Water Board office. During the war, the staff members contributed to a periodic cash collection to establish a fund that would obtain and/or purchase suitable items to make up parcels of comfort to send to those staff members who were in the Services. As no addresses were available for Mr. L and me, the money that would have been used for our parcels was kept aside and eventually used to purchase National Savings Certificates in our names. The purpose of the meeting was therefore to present our certificates to us. I cannot recall the value of our certificates, but they were highly acceptable.

The meeting was held in the boardroom, and a speech was given welcoming us home. All very pleasant. I was presented with my gift first, and I hope I made a suitable short speech of thanks. Mr. L, who had returned from a remote place in the Far East the day before, was then presented with his. His speech was short and to the point: "Very many thanks indeed for the certificates," he said. Before adding, "But you will have to excuse me - I must p*** off now, I'm going to a wedding." There was little rehabilitation required there.

Chapter 36

Rehabilitation and the RAF

I soon settled into my new job, but was still bothered about this inability to settle down psychologically. This was evidenced by how I greatly upset my Sergeant one day when he came into my office waving a piece of paper. It was an instruction to the effect that a Canadian Dodge snowplough was to be delivered to the civilian authorities at Northolt in the Greater London area. He wanted to deliver it, but I told him I would. He was a permanent Air Force chap and was proud of his ability to drive all sorts of vehicles - large and small - and the snowplough was indeed a large vehicle. He obviously didn't think much of my out-ranking him, and I duly set off in the cumbersome thing. By the time I reached the top of Shap Fell, it was clear that the thing was losing water, and I had to stop regularly to refill the radiator. I called home and spent the night there, and the next day, I continued on my journey.

I got very bored with its misbehaviour and decided to call in at Tilstock for a day or two. It was here that I decided to leave the vehicle with my old Mechanical Transport Section, along with the attendant papers, and instructed them to attend to the repairs and then deliver it to Northolt. I returned to Crosby by train. I was still in a rebellious mood, and thus, after a great deal of thought, I was prompted to apply to get back in the air. I discovered that to accomplish this, I had to commit to an additional eighteen months. This suited me very well, and as far as my complete rehabilitation was concerned, it was probably one of the best decisions I ever made. I was ordered to attend an interview at RAF Headquarters in Bushy Park, in the Teddington area, not far from Twickenham.

I was interviewed by a Wing Commander, who, strangely enough, knew all about Linosa, as he had been stationed at Malta for a time, and said that he had been responsible for alerting the Navy, which organised a small landing force to get me off the island. But, as I have already stated, an aerial recce saw the remains of my Spitfire and was under the impression that I could not have possibly lived through the crash landing. They, therefore, instructed the naval landing party to return to Malta.

However, it was a pleasant interview, and he asked me which aircraft I would like to fly now that I was returning to the air. I had been thinking about this and recalling my experience with aircraft having only one engine, I said that I would very much like a change, and perhaps fly a plane called the De Havilland Hornet. These were scaled-down Mosquito single-seaters, twin-engine fighters. Quite fast with the two Merlin engines. He said he would organise it, but considering that I had not flown for a couple of years - and in any case, I had no twin-engine experience, he would get me a few hours dual on a Mosquito, and to that end, he would get me posted to RAF Linton on Ouse, near York for my bit of instruction. I left and took the train back to Crosby-on-Eden. Imagine my surprise when I found that I had been posted yet again. My prowess as a Mechanical Transport Officer must have spread, goodness knows why, and I had been posted to York to take up my new post of Group Mechanical Transport Officer. It was a Squadron Leader post, but needless to say, I remained a Flight Lieutenant - and my pay remained the same!

I arrived at Group Headquarters to find that there was no accommodation in the Mess, or more accurately, there was a little, but this was reserved for those of a much higher rank than me, and the place seemed to be swarming with them. I was given a list of names and addresses of people who provided board and lodging, and set off on a bicycle to choose one. I disregarded the first few on sight and eventually chose a quite nice-looking house, which I was accepted as a lodger. It turned out that three females were living there: two sisters, one of whom was married to a Canadian airman who was waiting to go to Canada. The other sister was a widow whose sixteen-year-old girl was the third person. They looked after me very well, and we had some good laughs. As an officer, I was responsible for buying my uniform, and since the trousers and blouse given to me at Cosford were not really formal attire, I had purchased a second-hand uniform. It carried the Pilot's Wings and the correct rank, and that was all. I did not bother to organise the medal ribbons for it, and this was apparently a mistake. The collection of Officers in the Ante-Room, having drinks before dinner, was somewhat different from the norm. Being the Headquarters, there was a preponderance of high-ranking officers. I had been in the ante-room a short while and had got a beer when a Wing Commander came up to me and informed me that the Air Commodore wished to speak to me.

I supposed I was a new face, and he would want to know what I was doing at his Headquarters. I followed the Wing Commander. "Flight Lieutenant," he said, "Are you not entitled to wear any Medal Ribbons?" he asked. I replied that I was, upon which he ordered me to appear the next evening with them sewn on. I obtained the Ribbons and found a friendly lady from the Women's Auxiliary Air Force who assisted me with the sewing. I duly reported to the Air Commodore the following evening. "That's better, Flight Lieutenant," he said, "wear them always and be proud of them." "Yes, Sir," I replied and moved away.

Life at Group Headquarters was enjoyable, and my Staff consisted of a Sergeant and an Airman clerk. I had a car and driver at my disposal whenever I needed them. Perhaps my apparent success as a Mechanical Transport Officer was because I had decided from the start that I had to approach the job in my fashion. I decided that, as the war in Europe was now over, arrangements should be made to propose a scheme to the Station Officers at Tilstock and Crosby to remove from the establishment any vehicles that were not used frequently, except for those required for emergencies, such as Fire and ambulance services. This seemed to go down well, so I decided to pursue this line and went through the establishment lists for each station under my jurisdiction. I sent out amended established lists to each Station Commander and waited for their replies. It is strange to say, but these were accepted on the whole. It was also, the Sergeant told me, that it was my job to visit these RAF Stations in the Group and make an inspection.

This, too, was a lovely job. I was driven to a Station of my choice and reported in at the main gate Guard Room. I then proceeded to the Mechanical Transport Section, where I was usually joined by the Station Adjutant, who would be keen to make the tour of inspection as short as possible and would inform me that lunch was available. We would adjourn to the bar and, after a few beers, would partake of lunch. After that, I would make a few complimentary remarks, take my leave, and be driven back to York in a slightly bemused state. I would send a report to my superior stating that I had visited the Station. As I said, life was pleasant, but I still had the desire to get back into the air as soon as possible. I did not have to wait long at all, and my posting to Linton-on-Ouse came through. This was for a few hours in a Mosquito.

I never received my instruction as a further posting came in, not for a Hornet squadron, but for a squadron at RAF Horsham St. Faith. This was just outside Norwich. I arrived there to find that the squadron was a rather peculiar setup. It had a few Spitfires, a couple of Hawker Henleys, an Oxford or two, and a little Miles Magister.

The squadron's duties were those of cooperation. In other words, a sort of dogsbody outfit. And now, on looking back, a rather strange thing happened. Apart from the short trip I had enjoyed with Douglas up at Millfield, I had not flown for over two years, but nobody seemed to know this, as I had been posted there as an experienced Spitfire pilot. I suppose that I felt a certain amount of trepidation as I climbed into the Spitfire for my first trip. But it was just as though I had never left the cockpit, and I took off without any trouble at all. My duty was to fly backwards and forwards on a particular course along the coastline of Norfolk at a precise height and speed. This was to give the gunners on the ground practice with their predictors. The predictor was a rather primitive electronic device that, when aimed at the aircraft, would display the course, height, and speed of the aircraft. This information was relayed to the adjacent gunner, who had a Bofors anti-aircraft gun that fired shells set to explode at a specified height. The fact that in these exercises, they didn't fire any shells, to say the least, was comforting.

After about an hour of this, I would return to base. I made it known that I wished to take any job that would give me more airtime. I hoped that perhaps I would be able to expand my repertoire by gaining some flight time in the twin-engine Oxford or the Anson - this latter being an aircraft that had been used for a long time for training Navigators. But it was not to be. The only other job I got was to fly the Hawker Henley. This was the largest single-engine machine, which was very much underpowered, and it lumbered along. It had been fitted with a hook in the tail for towing a drogue. I was told about the method used for takeoff and for releasing the drogue before landing. I suppose the towing cable was about fifty yards long. Before landing, one flew low alongside the runway, pulled the release lever, and, on the following circuit, landed the aircraft. Off I went in the Henley, picked up the drogue, and was followed by a couple of Spitfires for target practice. These were flown by pilots under operational training and were, of course, very enthusiastic, especially as they were fully armed. Upon my return, the drogue was inspected to determine how many holes they had managed to puncture in it. I found this to be a rather unpleasant job. The Spitfire pilots were naughty boys and did not always keep to attacks from the side of the quarter, but occasionally from dead astern. I warned them, over the radio, that if they persisted in this stupidity, I would drop the drogue anywhere, thus saving my own skin. The war was over, and I was not going to be shot down now at this late stage. On returning to base, I would give them a right old lecture and tell them that if they persisted in such behaviour, then I would refuse to be a sitting duck for them. Otherwise, I was enjoying the flying practice myself and managed to get home for a couple of weeks. Out of the blue came another posting. This time, I was to report to RAF Burtonwood near Warrington, for onward transmission overseas!

It took me only a few seconds to convince myself that I wasn't having that one, so I immediately went to the Station Orderly Room and asked a clerk to put me through to Air Ministry, Section P2, which was the Officers' Postings. I told whoever answered the phone my Number, Rank, and Name, and informed them that I was a returned POW and had not yet been back in the UK for the specific period, as I was not yet able to be posted overseas. I told him that I would wait to hear from him. The reply came extremely quickly. I had hardly returned to the Flight Office when a message came through that Flight Lieutenant Cam would report to the Station Commander's Office immediately. This was indeed an action, and I felt very pleased that I had acted so quickly. I was shown into the Station Commander's Office, and as I saluted, I recognised him. He had been a Wing Commander in Stalag Luft III. Great - I thought.

He spoke in a stern tone. "So you are the officer who took the liberty of telephoning Air Ministry?" "Yes, Sir." "Well, Flight Lieutenant, you are posted—go to it. Dismissed". And that was that.

It was evident that I was not allowed to speak, and so I saluted and left. Rather disgruntled, I returned to the Flight Office. The arrival date at Burtonwood gave me a couple of possible days at home, so I packed my kit and left—so much for Horsham St. Faith.

Chapter 37

On the Move - Yet Again

I had enjoyed my couple of days at home, and my new Brother-in-Law said he would accompany me in my car to Burtonwood and return to Blackpool, where I said he was quite at liberty to use the car in my absence.

He dropped me at the main gate - in I went, and he turned for home. I booked in and established that my posting was for RAF Udine, located near Treviso in northeastern Italy. The route was designated to travel by train to Euston, then on to Dover and across the Channel to Calais, and thence by MEDLOC*. Now, the word MEDLOC stood for initials that I have long since forgotten, but it was a troop train that ran from Calais down to Treviso, thence down the east coast of Italy through Rimini, and then across the country to Rome and finally to Naples. Then, it returned along the same route. It ran day and night, but didn't stop at recognised railway stations; instead, it stopped at Army Feeding Posts. Everyone left the train to be washed and fed, and then the train resumed its journey. It was a somewhat weary journey.

However, we boarded the train at Warrington, and I found myself in

---

* MEDLOC was the official route and process used to evacuate wounded soldiers from active theatres of war (especially in Europe) back to the UK for further treatment and recovery. It stood for "Medical Location".

charge of a party of Airmen - a Flight Sergeant, a couple of Sergeants and Corporals, and about a dozen Airmen. Once the train had started, I handed the papers to the Flight Sergeant and informed him that he was in charge of the party, then promptly left him to it. We crossed London and boarded the train for Dover. It is somewhat of an admission, but after that, I never saw the rest of the party again. I always presumed that they had reached their destination - but quite honestly, I didn't care. We were a party of four or five Officers, all pilots, and made the journey as comfortable as possible. It was on this journey that I learned to play the game of solo.

We spent the night in Dover Castle, of all places. Crossed the Channel the next day and joined MEDLOC. It was now late November or early December 1945, and we disembarked at Treviso and were taken by lorry to our new aerodrome at Udine.

The squadron was short of Spitfire pilots, so that was the reason for the exercise. We were told that Marshal Tito, the self-appointed dictator of Yugoslavia, was beginning to assert his authority, and our job was to fly over that country and "wave the flag" to show our presence.

In our spare time, we took a trip to Venice, where we stayed in a requisitioned hotel - the finest in the city at the time. I also tried skiing in Cortina, but this turned out to be a waste of time for me. An attempt at the sport many years later proved equally unsuccessful!

Just before Christmas, an order came through to ground all the Spitfires and to re-equip with North American Mustang aircraft. I found these to be a very pleasant fighter to fly and quite fast. We continued with the same job.

I was approached one day by the Squadron Leader, who asked me if I would like to spend Christmas in London. Without hesitation, I agreed, and he then said that he would have overload petrol tanks fitted to two Mustangs, and we would give it a try.

The two of us took off and flew on an approximate course to Paris. We had been going for a while when he called me on the radio. "How high are the Alps?" he questioned. I racked my brain and tried to recall my school day's geography. "About seventeen thousand feet," I said, and asked, "Have you not got a map?" He said he had and held it up to the cockpit hood. It was, believe it or not, a Boots Diary, and all Europe was on a page about three inches square! You can perhaps imagine my thoughts, but I said nothing. As we flew northwest, the weather became very nasty, and we were practically flying in clouds. Sometime later, and by mutual consent, we reluctantly turned back and landed at Udine with not a great deal of petrol left. So that was the trip to London for Christmas!

We were into the New Year when the squadron was disbanded. The hierarchy considered the job to be complete, and all the pilots were posted to Villach, Austria, for onward transmission. Here we were joined by other Spitfire lads from another Station in Austria. We had nothing to do except wait for our postings. Villach was a small town, and it was in the local hotel - the Hotel Poste that I met Ivy Benson and her Ladies' Band. We spent every evening there before returning to our residence. It wasn't many days before a List of Postings was pinned to the Notice Board. The postings were for various locations, including the UK. All the pilots were posted except for a chap named Syd Walker and me. It was here that I met my friend Johnny Woodside, with whom I would later be stationed. There was a big party in the Mess the night before they all left, and the next morning, they saw a certain amount of damage left in their wake.

Syd and I were presented with a bill for the damage, which we immediately disposed of, informing the officer in charge of the Mess that he would need to send a portion of the bill to all concerned if he wanted payment. We never heard any more. Two days later, the postings for Syd and me came through. I was destined for Abu Sueir in Egypt to await instructions from Air Headquarters Jerusalem, and so was Syd. We joined the MEDLOC train again, and upon arriving in Rimini, we decided to drop off and spend a couple of days there. And so we did, and then we joined MEDLOC again for Rome, where we were to catch a flight to Egypt.

On arrival in Rome, we were taken to the requisitioned Officers' hotel—a five-star establishment called Hotel Reale, where we met the rest of the Villach lads who were destined for the Middle East. The scheme was that each day, we were supposed to contact the airport to see if there were any vacancies on flights to Egypt. We were given a priority number, but it was not the highest priority. This suited us fine, and we had a great time in Rome. Believe it or not, we neglected to inquire about vacant seats at the airport for some days. My friend

Johnny was there, and I was still with Syd, so we were pretty happy. Each evening, we would go to a nearby restaurant and enjoy the same meal every night. Meal prices were fixed and remarkably cheap. The first course was spaghetti with butter and parmesan cheese.

This was followed by half a chicken, then steak, with several fried eggs on top. The whole lot was, of course, washed down with wine. Leaving there, we walked to a nearby nightclub called the Colibri, where we stayed until the small hours. High living indeed! But all things come to an end, and we tired of our stay in Rome. We tried hard, and eventually, about half a dozen of us got a lift - I think - in the DC3, where we all sat on the floor. On that trip, we went through an electric thunderstorm, which was not very pleasant.

We had been in Egypt for only a day or two when my posting came through to RAF Ein Shemer, near Haifa in Palestine (now, of course, called Israel). Johnny was posted to the same squadron (No. 32), and Syd was posted to Cyprus. We were never questioned about our lateness in arriving, so all was well. At Ein Shemer, I was back on the March IX Spitfire - a very nice aeroplane.

I would say that after the 1914-1918 war, Great Britain was given a mandate to rule and administer Palestine, a role it had been fulfilling since the early 1920s. The Army was present, and the British Palestine Police Force controlled the country under the terms of the mandate. Specifically, it stipulated, among other things, that immigration into Palestine was to be strictly limited. But, and it was a big but, the European Jews, who had suffered such awful atrocities under the Hitler regime, were determined to have a country of their own and had decided to establish themselves in Palestine.

Their forebears came from there, and to this end, they availed themselves of every means to secure a journey from mainland Europe to Palestine. However, Great Britain was required to adhere to the Terms of the Mandate until 1948. You can imagine the poor homeless Jews setting sail from places like Marseilles on every manner of ship that they could get hold of. Each boat was loaded down to the gunwales with bodies. A sort of war developed.

The Royal Navy patrolled the coast of Palestine about a hundred miles out, looking for these immigrant ships. They would board them against extremely vicious opposition and endeavour to turn them back.

The RAF bombers would patrol about fifty miles out, and we would patrol the actual coastline. Those who managed to get through to the coast would land and be met by the British Army, who would take them prisoner. When we, in our Spitfires, found an immigrant ship, we would report its position and fly low over it to try and assess how many immigrants were aboard. This was, of course, impossible, and volleys of rifle fire would meet us. Needless to say, our hierarchy decreed that we would not be provided with any ammunition. I suppose the best we could do was to stick our tongues out at them!

It was a funny sort of war to be involved in, and many were killed on both sides. Our aerodrome was constantly attacked by mortar and rifle fire. The so-called enemy was, until a very short time before, on our side of the fence against a common enemy - Hitler. So, it was not a war but a Police Force action against those who were breaking the law at the time. We, the British, had to carry on with the job of policing and administering the country of Palestine according to the Mandate we had been given thirty years before.

It is my humble opinion to this day that the Jews were wrong in pouring into Palestine and saying that this country is now ours and is called Israel. The Mandate finished in the year after I left (1948), when they came in their thousands. The Arabs who had cohabited the land with some Jews since Biblical times, and before, were kicked out of parts of Palestine or shepherded into sort of refugee camps, where some of them remain to this day. The invasion by the Jews and their attempt to dominate started a conflict between Jews and Arabs, and it is still carrying on now, fifty years later. It would seem that an unsolved problem has been created.

So, this was now my new job, a sort of Flying Policeman on constant patrol. We also patrolled the Syrian border, and here again, we encountered fire from the opposing side. Don't ask me why; ask the Foreign Office. Another patrol route was along the oil pipeline, which was laid above ground and ran from Haifa to Baghdad.

Chapter 38

Palestinian Incidents

I found life in Palestine to be quite pleasant, and I once again thoroughly enjoyed flying. It seemed that I was as much at home in the cockpit of a Spitfire as I was on the ground. We were kept busy with our jobs, but I was introduced to the game of squash, which I took to immediately and played twice a day. Tennis was also available, and I thoroughly enjoyed it as well. All these amenities, of course, were located on the airfield, and we were more or less confined to the camp. It was dangerous to walk about outside, as some of the Jewish boys would shoot at the sight of a uniform. However, I did manage to see parts of Haifa, Jerusalem, Jericho, Bethlehem, and Nazareth, and I also took a swim in the Sea of Galilee. All were well-known names from youth, and the only place to which entry was restricted was Jerusalem, which had barbed wire fences everywhere. I would never visit any of the places alone, and we were constantly on the lookout for any untoward happening. But luckily, I was never accosted or attacked.

Ken in Palestine, 1947

The duty of Officer of the Guard came around occasionally. It meant being stationed in the Guard House's front gate for a twenty-four-hour period, ensuring that all guards departed on time and were properly manning their posts. Some were single guards in posts around the perimeter of the airfield. When visiting them, I was fascinated watching the giant praying mantis devouring all insects that came within reach of its extremely long and sticky tongue. On my first tour of duty as Officer of the Guard, I went into the sandbagged Main Gate guard post, which had two Airmen, each in charge of a Browning 303 machine gun. These were the machine guns used in the Spitfire, and I knew them inside out. We had learned the various reasons why a gun would stop firing and the immediate cure. I said to the two Airmen: "What would you do if you had a number two stoppage on your gun?"

They both looked at me as though I were speaking some foreign tongue. I questioned them further and established that they had received absolutely no instruction in the use of a Browning machine gun - or any other gun for that matter. I submitted a report in strong terms to the Station Commander regarding this matter. I was right, of course, but he didn't like my report and told me so. There was nothing wrong with the report - it was the fact that he was, in the end, responsible for all matters that happened at his Station.

Nevertheless, I was convinced that the matter was serious and should be reported so that something could be done about it. This was the first time I met the Station Commander, a comparatively elderly Group Captain who had been in the Air Force for yonks and was a stereotype of an administrative type. I very much doubt that he had ever been in an aeroplane in his life. I fully appreciate that one has to have the admin type, but their outlook was so utterly different from the rest of us. I do not doubt that he was desperate to return to the pre-war, peaceful style of life, some of which I was to experience over the next year or so. However, we had met, and I had made an unfavourable impression, so, in hindsight, I shall call this incident number one.

One of the pilots on the squadron, who hailed from Peckham, London, was called Vic. One day, his orders came through to return the next day via Egypt to the UK for demobilisation. He was a very likeable chap, and that very night, therefore, there was a party in the Mess. He was to leave very early the next morning. It was the usual type of Mess party - boisterous and hilarious, and the beer flowed continually. The gent's toilet was some distance away across the large lawn. After daylight, it was pretty standard, although strictly forbidden, for the lads to "water the lawn" rather than waste time walking right across the lawn and back. I have to say now, very guiltily, that I was watering the lawn on this occasion, but at least I was behind a tree. Unfortunately, the tree moved away. It turned out to be the Squadron Leader! As he was in the same carefree state as the rest of us, the matter was never referred to again. I trust that he did not get rheumatism in the leg as a result of the episode.

Later that evening, before the party ended, Vic wrote the following words on the wall of the bar parlour with a pencil: "Let me introduce you to the Fighting 32nd" and signed it. About a dozen others followed his signature. You could say then that this was behaviour unbefitting of an officer and a gentleman. I agree - it was, and the high-ranking Officers thought so as well. Consequently, the next day, five of us were summoned to the Group Captain's office. The signatures of the five of us were the only ones that could be recognised. Johnny Woodside and I, along with three others whose names I have forgotten, stood in line in front of his desk to receive a telling-off in no uncertain terms. We were, of course, questioned about the name of the instigator of this awful act. No one spoke, of course, knowing full well that if Vic's name were mentioned, he would be dragged back from Egypt, where he was waiting for a flight to the UK. The Group Captain ranted on and finished by calling us a gutless lot. I wasn't having that and said that I was in possession of a Flight Log Book, which would disprove his statement. He stared at me and then dismissed us all, but he had seen my face again—incident number two.

I was dispatched one day with my number two, Johnny, on some job or other, and on the way out to our aircraft, I suggested that we should see how quickly we could get airborne. We taxied off at no mean speed, and I was in front. As I rounded the corner of a hangar, I was confronted by a parked aircraft. An Airman was working on it, and I screeched to a halt. My wing tip hit the wing tip of the parked aircraft, and the terrified Airman jumped off. Johnny also screeched to a halt behind me. I got out and found that there was no damage whatsoever, so I climbed back in and took off. However, the incident was reportable, and on my return, I did just that. I was told that the incident would be reported to the Station Commander—incident number three.

MAKE IT DO

I suppose that he would chunter to himself: "Not that fellow again!" However, I heard no more about it. The following incident involved a routine practice flight for Johnny and me. Nothing untoward about that, but I had heard somewhere, sometime, about a place called Petra - the rose-red city half as old as time.

It sounded very interesting, indeed, so I proposed taking a look at it. If you look at a map of Palestine and Trans Jordan of the 1940's era, you will see that apart from areas to the west of the River Jordan, which flows down from the Sea of Galilee to the Dead Sea and on to its outlet at Aqaba, the whole area is just a splodge of varying shades of brown. Petra was not marked. However, I thought I knew approximately where it would be, so we set off in a south-easterly direction. You know what it is like. "I'll try a bit further south or east or whatever," but I didn't see it. Having seen pictures of the place since, it certainly would not be easy to see from the air unless you were practically on top of it. It's somewhat surprising, but it has now become a tourist destination. We turned for home. In hindsight, I realised I had gone too far east.

Johnny was on the radio saying that he was running very low on petrol. I told him which engine revs to select and the most economical engine boost to employ, and we reduced speed to the most economical level. This was getting a bit serious, but we flew on for about another quarter of an hour or so when he called to say: "I'm out of petrol. Shall I bail out?" "No," I said: "Put it into a gentle glide at about 135/140 mph and maintain this course." We had sufficient height to continue for a time, and lo and behold, I spotted a landing strip in the middle of nowhere. "Belly land it on that strip," I said, and coached him down. "Don't forget: wheels up, not down." He made a very good landing, and as soon as the aircraft stopped, he jumped out and waved. I had told him that I would get help, and when I saw he was alright, I flew off to the nearest aerodrome, a place near the coast called Aquir. I landed and reported the incident, and they immediately dispatched a jeep to pick him up. They said they would retrieve the aircraft at a later date. I refuelled and returned to Ein Shemer. They were not happy at all with my tale of woe, and I was quickly informed that although I myself had not run out of petrol, I was in charge, and it was, therefore, my fault. Another unfortunate incident to add to my character, which was beginning to become rather cloudy, to say the least.

Around this time, someone in the hierarchy decided that it would be a good idea to arm the Spitfires with one bomb of about eleven pounds. Now, I don't know who decided that my aircraft should be the one to act as a guinea pig. I had my suspicions that it was I and not the aircraft that was chosen. So, the armourers went to work and fitted the bomb, complete with the release lever, in the cockpit. I was told that the aircraft was ready, so I went along and was shown how to release the bomb. A target had been chosen for me, and I took off. I must admit that I didn't fancy the trip very much, but there we are. I found the target and put the plane into a dive, heading straight for it. At the specified height, I pulled the bomb release lever and pulled up and around to see how accurate I had been. There was no explosion! What on earth had happened? It soon became apparent that the bomb was still there under the aircraft. This was serious. I would have to make the smoothest, most gentle landing I had ever done; otherwise, if the bomb released on landing, it would blow the aircraft up and me with it. I called the base and told them what had happened. Someone said, "Best of luck!"

As I approached the runway, I could see that quite a crowd had gathered to witness the landing. I put all my flying knowledge into that landing and was extremely relieved when there was no explosion. I gently braked, and as soon as the aircraft stopped, I was out and running. I played stink with the armourers and told them to go out to the aircraft and deal with the bomb, and I watched from a distance. They released the bomb safely, and that was the end of that. I thought afterwards that I might have been congratulated or received a few kind words from the Squadron Commander - but no.

I seemed to be the target for hazardous trips because a couple of days after the bomb trial, I was ordered by the CO to deliver in person a letter to Air Headquarters at Jerusalem. The weather was atrocious, and I made that clear. Nevertheless, he said, "That's the order." It was unusual for Palestine, but the cloud was well below the mountain tops, which I had to cross to reach a particular flat valley with a landing strip that served as the nearest airstrip to Jerusalem. The landing strip ran east-west and crossed the roadway, which ran north from Jerusalem. More by good luck than good management, I found it as I came through the cloud. At the sight of an aircraft, an Airman would close the roadway by lowering two barriers to give precedence to the plane. I felt relieved to have found the place and landed, and then asked for transport to Air Headquarters, where I delivered my letter. I returned to the refuelled aircraft and took off, finding the flight back much easier. Was it a necessary and urgent job? I wondered. Once again, I had beaten them!

I suppose that by now, we were getting towards the end of 1946, and the conflict with the immigrating Jews was continuing, as indeed it would until the time came for the Mandate to end. It was peaceful, yet it was wartime and could be quite hazardous, to the extent that we were awarded a "Palestine Medal" to add to our collection of Campaign Ribbons. I said it was peaceful and, as such, peacetime procedures in the RAF were being quickly revived. One facet of these was that a confidential report on each officer was made every six months. These were written by the Squadron Leader and forwarded to the Air Ministry via the Station Commander. If the report was good, then nothing was heard of it; however, if the report, as described, was adverse, then the officer had to read it and sign it. I have no idea what the consequences of that would be.

However, one day, the Group Captain sent for me and informed me that he had received a confidential report about me, which contained adverse information. This, I must admit, shook me somewhat. Although I was going through a rebellious period, I never expected this. He told me to read it and sign it. I read that I was guilty of leading Junior Officers astray and that my behaviour as a pilot was poor. The report concluded that this officer keeps himself very fit. The Group Captain told me to sign it. I refused, saying that I disagreed with the report. He babbled something about a court-martial - but I ignored it. After all, I may have been a bit boisterous and devil-may-care, but I was no criminal. After expressing his disappointment, he dismissed me and informed me that I would hear further on the matter. After a couple of days, I was in front of him again. The report had been rewritten, and although I was not entitled to read it, as it was no longer adverse, he allowed me to do so. I read it, smiled, and said, "Thank you, sir." Why the change of heart, I wondered.

All in all, I thought it was perhaps time I sought adventure elsewhere. Now, Baghdad had always conjured up in my mind pictures of palaces, the Arabian Nights, and veiled dancing girls. I knew that there was an RAF Station near Baghdad called Habbaniya. I did not know what type of aircraft they had, but I nevertheless applied for a posting there.

To finalise the chapter on Palestine, there is one more story to add. As I mentioned earlier, we were flying Spitfires of the Mark IX type, which were significantly more powerful than the Mark V. They had a four-blade propeller and a larger engine and were indeed a very nice plane to fly.

Ken and the Spitfire Mark IX in Palestine

The squadron received a signal that some Spitfire XVIII aircraft had been shipped to Egypt from the UK in crates, and the first one was almost ready for a test flight. So, who did you think they chose for this onerous test flight? They chose the pilot who was the most experienced Spitfire pilot around - also the pilot whose performance in the air apparently left a lot to be desired! Obviously, it was a load of rubbish that they had written about me, because when the first serious job of test flying came along, they chose me! I felt quite elated to be the first pilot in the Middle East to fly a Mark XVIII.

I got an aircraft down to Abu Sueir in the Canal Zone of Egypt. The flight there was somewhat different. It was in a two-seater passenger plane, similar to the present-day two-seaters used for flight training, such as an Auster or Chipmunk. The aircraft was alright - it was the pilot who was a bit off. He had been to a party the night before and was hardly awake. Flight Lieutenant Woods, if I remember.

He managed to concentrate sufficiently to take off, and we headed down the coast of Palestine at about one thousand feet. I spent the whole flight with my eyes glued on him, and I cannot remember the number of times I had to shake him awake. A disastrous flight, to say the least. He sincerely thanked me after we landed for seeing him through, and he headed for his bed. So much for Flight Lieutenant Woods.

I found the hangar where this first Mark XVIII was nearing completion, and I made myself known. I looked at this brand-new aircraft. It was superb and larger than the Mark IX. It had a much more powerful engine and a five-blade propeller. It had four cannons, a more bulbous Perspex hood for improved visibility, and a significantly greater range, thanks to its usual main petrol tank located between the cockpit and engine, as well as additional tanks in the wings. I sat in the cockpit and surveyed the instruments and cockpit layout. This was much the same with additions such as a multi-purpose fuel cock to switch from one tank to another. The Flight Sergeant gave me a booklet entitled "Pilot's Notes," which I read through earnestly. It noted the takeoff and landing speeds, stalling speed, and other relevant information. It would, I was told, be at least two or three days before they had completed their work and run it up to test the engine.

Having booked in, I decided to visit a small place called Ismalia, located in the Canal Zone and north of the Great Bitter Lake, which forms part of the Suez Canal. At Ismalia, there was an Officers' Rest Centre, and it was, by comparison to the surrounding Stations, quite picturesque. Surrounded by trees, it was close to the sweet water canal; swimming in this small canal was prohibited because of leeches and another sort of 'tick', which burrowed into the skin and sucked blood. However, I enjoyed seeing the small town and spent a couple of days there.

Arriving back at Abu Sueir, I was told that the Spitfire would be ready to test fly the next morning. Should everything be OK, I was then to fly it back to Ein Shemer and the squadron. I went down there after breakfast and saw that they had pushed it out of the hangar. I signed the sheet to indicate that I had inspected the completion signatures of the fitters, riggers, radio mechanics, etc. I climbed in, fitted the parachute straps and aircraft harness straps, started it up, and called the Control Tower on the radio. "All clear to taxi," they said. So I gently taxied to the end of the runway and again called up the tower for permission to take off. Given the all-clear, I taxied onto the far end of the runway, lined it up, and opened the throttle—quite a difference in the amount of power. As soon as it was airborne, I raised the wheels and began to climb. I made a couple of wide circuits around the aerodrome and then climbed to about 10,000 feet.

It certainly was a lovely machine, and I felt quite at home. I put it through some manoeuvres, but nothing too fierce. I flew around for about half an hour, testing all the functions and monitoring all the gauges. A superb aeroplane! I brought it back to the circuit and asked for permission to land. Having studied the "Pilot's Notes" (which booklet, believe it or not, I still have somewhere), I knew the approach speed and stalling speed. I came over the boundary fence and prepared for touch-down, and then came the shock!

It would not touch down, but just kept floating along a few feet above the runway. I opened the throttle, climbed again, and reported to the Control Tower that the thing would not sit down. I went round again and approached the runway at as low a speed as I dared. The same thing happened. It would not sit down. I told the Control Tower that I would try again. I came in again as slow as I dared - but no success! On the fourth attempt, I employed the powered approach, which involved bringing it in nose up and on full power. Theoretically, when the engine power was shut off, the plane would drop like a brick. Success! The aircraft sank onto the runway. As I was speeding along the runway, I breathed a sigh of relief - but not for long, for as I applied the brakes, there was absolutely no response. I pulled the brake lever on and off, but to no avail. There was absolutely nothing I could do except call up the tower and say, "No brakes!"

I went off the end of the runway into the sand, and the aircraft dug its nose and propeller into the sand. The fire engine and ambulance had been alerted, and as I jumped out, they arrived. I had switched off everything, so there was no fire, and I was completely unhurt.

Back at the hanger, I told them the weary tale in no uncertain manner. I reported to the officer in charge of the Maintenance Unit, who had done the rebuild, and told my story. The news spread quickly, of course, and I was soon informed that I was not to leave the site until I had attended a Court of Inquiry.

A Court of Inquiry is a semi-formal affair, and I found on arrival that the court consisted of two Squadron Leaders - both non-fliers. This disappointed me as they introduced themselves. They asked me to tell them exactly what had happened, so I did, and they listened intently. Then came the first question, which amazed me. "How many crew did I have?" I could not believe that a serving RAF officer did not know the answer to that one. I pondered a moment and said: "Gentlemen, if you have to ask me a question like that about the most famous RAF Fighter, then I hardly think you are capable of assessing me as a pilot, or the possible faults in the aircraft. I therefore request that another court be convened. "Well, Flight Lieutenant, that is your right, and I will report your request."

I left, and the same afternoon, I was told that another court had been convened, which I was supposed to attend. This time, one of the people in the court was a flying type, and we went through the proceedings again. I managed to get an airlift back to Palestine the next day, and in the meantime, I went to the maintenance hangar, but they had yet to find any faults.

I returned to Ein Shemer, and you can imagine the stir and annoyance about what had happened. It was not as bad as I thought it would be. It was a terrible shame, really, and I felt awful about it, but I could not see that I had made any mistakes. It had been a lovely flight, and I had taken the aircraft up to just under forty thousand feet, which was its ceiling. I had never been that high before, and it felt very lonely indeed. The old Mark V would get up to below thirty thousand feet, and the Mark IX a couple of thousand above that. But forty thousand feet was pretty high for those days.

I returned to routine patrol work and practice flying, and soon, I was informed that my fellow pilot, Pilot Officer Bell, and I would be granted a weekend of leave. We were then allowed to take an aircraft and spend a couple of days in Cyprus. Wonderful. We took off, and I set a course for Famagusta aerodrome at the eastern end of that island.

The island was not split into Turkish and Greek halves as it is today. Famagusta now lies in the sort of forbidden Turkish Sector. We had been flying a very short time when Ground Control at Ein Shemer came on the radio. "Flight Lieutenant Cam to return to base immediately. Pilot Officer Bell to continue his flight". What on earth had happened now?

I landed back at Ein Shemer and went to see the CO. "Here's a signal," he said. "You are grounded until the Court of Inquiry has reached its conclusions." I think he felt pretty sorry for me. So, what the dickens do I do now? How long are they going to take? I didn't have to wait long for the next thing to happen.

The Group Captain Station Commander sent for me. I was beginning to wear a hole in his mat! "You are posted as Flight Lieutenant," he said. "I am sending you to a friend of mine who will find you something to do. "Where am I going?" I asked. "You are posted to RAF Amman in Trans-Jordan," he replied.

I packed my kit and set off by road.

Chapter 39

A Commendation - A Black Mark - and A Claim to Fame

Life in Amman, although somewhat limited in recreation, was quite pleasant. I quite enjoyed starting work early in the morning and finishing at lunchtime. We were not confined to the Station, and although there was not much to see, we occasionally went down to Amman and looked around the town. Sometimes, we would buy meat and the other necessary ingredients to make a curry on a Primus stove in one of the rooms late at night. These were very enjoyable, and someone would prepare a supper each week. My roommate, Dr Wilkinson, was a young, recently qualified doctor and joined in with everything that was going on.

One morning, the Station Commander sent a clerk to ask me if I would go in and see him. The result was quite surprising; as I entered his office, he said, "Congratulations, Flight Lieutenant," and handed me a piece of paper. It was a signal from Air Headquarters, Jerusalem. Wondering what on earth it was, I read it, and the contents told me that the Court of Inquiry concerning the Spitfire XVIII prang had reached its conclusion, and that I was entirely blameless. The reason for the brake failure had been found, and it was also established that certain weights which should have been secured in the tail end of the fuselage were not there - hence the landing problem. The signal further stated that Flight Lieutenant Cam was free to return to flying duties if deemed practical. I thanked the Group Captain, and he asked me to let him know whether or not I wished to return to flying.

I had never had any doubts about the outcome of the Inquiry, but at the same time, it was a relief to know their answer. I thought about the flying, which I had missed, but the urge to fly had diminished somewhat of late, and as I had less than a couple of months to do before the end of my extra eighteen months, I was inclined to refuse their offer. If I had known where they would send me, I might have made a different decision, but as I was having a pleasant time in Amman, I decided to say no and informed the Group Captain of my decision. "That's fine," he said, "the replacement Accounts Officer is on his way, but I have no doubt we can find you something to do while you are here." They certainly did. The jobs came thick and fast. There were four in all, and they arrived over the course of the same week.

The first was Cypher Office. The chap I was taking over from was leaving for the UK, and before he departed, he managed to give me about half an hour of tuition in coding and decoding. As far as I recall, I received only one coded signal, and that was from Jerusalem, which struck me at the time as somewhat of a farce. Unless, of course, they knew I was new to the job and were testing me out. It was a strange procedure. Carrying my signal in a special case, I collected an armed guard and set off on foot to a small brick building that was all alone, about a hundred yards or so from the nearest building alongside the aerodrome. When we arrived, I opened the steel door with my special key, let myself in, and locked the door behind me. The guard stood outside. Inside was a table, a chair, and a safe. There was no electricity, so at night, one would have to bring some light. I opened the safe and extracted a thick book containing pages of five-digit numbers. I then set to work decoding the series of numbers I had received and wrote out the signal. As I said, it was rather stupid and could have well been sent by telephone.

It was addressed to the Station Commander, who informed him that the Air Officer commanding the group would be arriving by air at Amman on a specific date and time. I then wrote out a message stating that I had received and understood the signal, and when I returned to the Orderly Room, I instructed a clerk to dispatch it. I then put the book away in the safe, picking up any scrap paper. I locked the safe, let myself out, and locked the door. I was escorted back to my office. Anyway, it was a good practice, but I never needed the knowledge again - that is, except to write about it here and now.

Job number two was the officer responsible for the Guard. This meant that I had to ensure guards were always on duty, as per the rosters I created. That is to say, not the Airmen - they were dealt with by the Sergeant, but the Officers on Guard Duty for twenty-four hours at a time. This was brilliant. I soon realised the enormous perk of this honourable position, and that was that I never put down my name. I had always hated guard duty, ever since my Ground School days in Newquay - although I had not done any since 1940 or 1941. So that was that number.

Job number three was the Office of the Keys. This one was even simpler. I held the very important keys, and when someone applied for a particular key, I assessed whether they should have it and whether I should accompany them. As simple as that.

Job number four was that of Mess Secretary. This, I suppose, was a thankless job. The worst part of it was extracting cash from the other Officers to pay their Mess Bills. But I can't say that it worried me very much - indeed, I did not lose any sleep over it. One night, my safe in the Mess Secretary's Office was broken into, and all the cash was stolen. Disaster! Luckily, at the time, there wasn't a great deal of money there. You may say there was nothing very strange about a robbery. That was very true—the strange bit was that there was an identical occurrence the night before at Ein Shemer in Palestine. Guess who the Mess Secretary was there at that time - none other than my old pal, Johnny Woodside. He suffered more than I did in that he was put on open arrest. This meant that he could not, under any circumstances, leave the Station and had to sign in at the Guard House four times every twenty-four hours. Did the two friendly Station Commanders of Ein Shemer and Amman get together on the phone, and did they suspect some collusion? After a couple of weeks, they let Johnny off the hook as they had arrested the Arab gang who were responsible for both robberies whilst they were having a go at an Army Station.

Now, we come to the black mark referred to in the title of this chapter. The Officers were invited to a buffet and dance to be held in a particular Church Hall in the town of Amman. The Church had a

Church of England (C. of E.) Vicar, and the church hall was also used as an infant school for children belonging mainly to the British Military. Palestine had been virtually run by the British since 1918, and there had also been strong ties between Trans-Jordan and Great Britain for many years. The King of Jordan, Abdullah, had been educated in England, as had his son, King Hussein.

There was a small three- or four-piece band, a buffet, and a bar. There were bout 40 or 50 people there, including Air Force and Army Officers and some local Arab dignitaries. I need hardly say that there was a dearth of females, mainly wives and chaperoned daughters of military personnel. The story of this dance is rather out of context and happened very shortly after I arrived in Trans-Jordan, and I offer that as a paltry excuse for what happened next.

The lady who ran this school was in her late fifties or early sixties, and seeing her somewhat at a loose end, I asked her if she would care to dance. She seemed very pleased to accept, and we started. She was very chatty and told me all about her work with the school. I asked her how long she had been there. She told me, but I cannot remember how many years she said. However, she then finished her sentence by saying that her connection to the country was that she was the Mother of Glubb Pasha. "Who is Glubb Pasha?" I said. She looked quite cross with me and said: "You've never heard of Glubb Pasha?" "I'm afraid not," I answered. Whereupon she dropped me as a partner and strode off to the Group Captain, and I could see her blazing away at him. What on earth had I done now?

I stood there awaiting developments, and the Group Captain came across to me. "I think you had better learn a little of the history of this country," he said. "But in the meantime, I suggest that you leave here and return to the Station," he added. "Yes, sir," and I beat a hasty retreat. How on earth was I supposed to know that Glubb Pasha was, in fact, a British Army officer, Major J.B. Glubb, who had been seconded to the Trans-Jordanian authorities and had formed the Arab Legion in 1923, trained in the British Army method? He eventually became the Chief of Staff of the Jordanian Army, a post he held until 1951. Not knowing these facts was the black mark. These black marks seemed to haunt me, and it really was a case of injured innocence. However, as they say, ignorance is no excuse in service life - so I hung my head in shame!

MAKE IT DO

Now we come to the final part of this chapter, which tells the story of what was—and probably still is — my only claim to fame. A message came through that Dr Wilkinson, whose rank I think was the same as mine, and I had to report to the Station Commander. We reported to him, and he told us that we had been invited, on a specific date, to be presented to and have lunch with no less than King Abdullah. This was big stuff indeed, and we looked forward to it! On the due date, a car and driver were laid on for us, and off we went to the Palace in Amman. We were greeted on arrival by a member of the Royal Household, a sort of Equerry, who led us to an antechamber. We waited there until all the guests had arrived. I think there would be about twenty in all. There were no ladies.

The Equerry put us in the picture. We would be presented to the King by Rank, Name, and Appointment. He told us that the King would not shake hands but would bow his head and that we must bow as well, but not in a dramatic manner.

We were ushered through double doors into the Reception Room and moved slowly in single file round to the side of the room towards the King. My turn came. "Flight Lieutenant Cam, Royal Air Force Station Amman," the Equerry said, and I stood in front of the King. He looked at me as though it were his job to remember my face till the day he died, and I remember his piercing eyes. We both bowed slightly, and I moved away.

The reception didn't take long, and we all went out onto the lawn where a marquee without sides had been erected. A long table was laid out, with chairs for all the guests. It was quite an interesting and perhaps awesome experience, but what followed was not so inviting.

The first course was soup, which in itself was palatable, but the fact that the tureen also held a few sheep's eyes rather put us off. However, we partook. The next course was lamb - or, more likely, mutton, and was carved from the whole animal. That was fine, but the entire thing was swarming with flies. The Doctor and I looked at each other. We agreed that we would have to eat, and so we did, vowing that at the first possible opportunity, we would make ourselves sick.

We were obviously of minor rank as we were sitting well away from the King, but I remember having the impression that he saw all that was going on. My impression was that he was a very nice chap, if one can describe a King in that manner, but also a very astute person.

As soon as we could leave the table, the Doctor and I made our way to a clump of trees at the edge of the lawn. We disappeared behind them and stuck our fingers down our throats! I only hope that guests at Buckingham Palace do not feel the need to behave in such an outrageous manner. However, apart from the gastronomical aspect of the occasion, I thought that I had had a very exalting experience. Although, as I have remarked, we were on the lower end of the dignitary scale. Nevertheless, we had been there and experienced royalty firsthand. So that was my claim to fame.

Chapter 40

The Journey Homewards

The decision not to return to flying for the short time before I was due to be demobilised seemed, on balance, to be the correct one. Life at RAF Amman was enjoyable, except perhaps for one facet which I have mentioned before. That was the apparent urgency to get things and routine back to peacetime practice. Whereas flying was once an important duty, it was now beginning to take a back seat and was being replaced by a bureaucratic administration, which I found rather annoying. To stick to the laid-down procedures instead of getting the job done was typical of a Government Department, which, of course, the Services were. Apart from that, I had done my time in the RAF and was firmly of the opinion that signing on for a further eighteen months was one of the better decisions I have ever made. I was now completely rehabilitated, which I had most certainly needed.

The extra period in the RAF had served as a stepping stone back to everyday civilian life. The possibility of applying for a permanent Commission was dispelled from my mind by the prospect of kowtowing to rank. That was certainly not in my nature. As far as I was concerned, people had to earn respect, not take it for granted. I always tried to apply this to myself when, in later years, I had the privilege of being part of a Management team.

Waiting in Egypt for a flight home

So, then, the time came for me to depart from Amman, and I was particularly pleased when the Station Commander wished me well and remarked that he had enjoyed my presence on the Station and that he was very sorry to see me go. And in a way, I was sorry myself. I had to wait for a visiting aircraft to give me a lift back to Egypt to a station called El Fayid on the Great Bitter Lake. After a few days, a plane arrived that was heading in the right direction. I cannot remember whether it was an Air Speed Oxford or an Avro Anson. In either case, it was a twin-engine passenger machine with a capacity of about a dozen. I was the only one travelling, so I joined the pilot at the sharp end (as they used to call it). It was a pleasant, routine flight, and I watched Trans-Jordan and Palestine slip by, wondering if I would ever be back there again. The Rose Red City, half as old as time - Petra - had eluded me, so perhaps one day I might get there.

We arrived at El Fayid, and I booked in. I would have to wait for a flight to the UK, but in the meantime, as I had just set foot in Egypt, I had to have an injection against Yellow Fever. That was nothing, but my face dropped a little when the Doctor told me that I would have to wait two weeks and then have a second jab. This came as a bit of a shock. I was now keyed up to getting home as soon as possible, and this boring fortnight had set me back. There was little to do except sit around, play tennis, and go swimming in the Great Bitter Lake. I also tried, for the first time in my life, sailing a yacht and found that occupation to be very pleasing, although I am certainly not a boat-minded person. I spent a couple of afternoons on the beach with a lady in her thirties. She was the daughter of an Army officer, and she delighted in the fact that there was a dearth of eligible females. Unfortunately, it looked (as they said in a cartoon) as though she had been hit with an ugly stick. But apart from that, she was pleasant company, as I said, and I got the impression that she desperately needed a partner, preferably for life.

MAKE IT DO

After about a week of this idle life, I had had enough. I forged my Medical Card with details of my second injection and presented myself at a Dispatch Office to get my name on the list for a flight. You may say that this bit of forgery was an unwise move and very disobedient, and I would probably agree with you. Luckily, I did not get Yellow Fever, so that was that. We all do silly things at times.

Having been added to the dispatch list, a flight arrived the next day. This was in the form of a big four-engined Avro York flying to the UK via Malta. The Avro York was a latecomer in the war, and I think it was designed as either a heavy bomber or a troop transport. However, this particular one was fitted out with seats. Don't get me wrong - they were not the type of seats you find in the modern airliner. Not by any means. It was a new aircraft, and, in light of what I have learned since, it was probably being flown back to the UK to be scrapped. Such is war! It would be much easier if, like a lot of things, you knew when they were going to end.

We took off and had been flying for about an hour when I once again grew a bit bored. I decided, therefore, to pay a visit to the sharp end. There was a crew of three or four who were playing cards! The aircraft was being flown by "George", the primitive automatic pilot. I was welcomed as a diversion and for a chat with the crew. I must mention here that many, many years later, I met a chap who was a pilot doing this sort of job, and he landed in the UK in one of these redundant aircraft and, having stepped out of the aircraft, was walking to the huts on the aerodrome. Before he was halfway there, a crane had gone alongside his charge and was swinging a large concrete ball at it and smashing it up! What sacrilege. After chatting with the crew, the Second Pilot was still at his post, so I asked the First Pilot if I could have a go at flying the thing. He readily agreed and took me into the pilot's seat. The instrument layout was fairly standard; the engine instruments, of course, were quadrupled, but most of the rest was fairly standard and "George" was disconnected. It was an interesting experience. Don't forget that I was used to flying very responsive fighters; that is, the response to the controls was immediate. On this lumbering aeroplane, the response was quite different and very, very slow. Occasionally, I was given an alteration, of course, but remained at the same height and speed.

It was enjoyable and far superior to sitting in the passenger seat. The navigator announced over the intercom that we were less than half an hour from Malta, and the Captain said that he would take over for the landing. I stayed in the cockpit area until we landed.

There was a short break here and time to have a cup of tea and a bun, so to speak, but as soon as the aircraft had been refuelled, we boarded, and it took off. I went back to my seat. There was no cabin pressurisation in those days, so we were flying at a comparatively low height - I suppose about six to eight thousand feet, and as we approached the south coast of France, daylight was beginning to fade. The rest of the journey was uneventful, and we landed at Lyneham. Now, there are two Lynehams - one in Wiltshire and one in Oxfordshire, but I am pretty certain that it was the one in Wiltshire. It matters not excepting that the next time I heard about the aerodrome was many, many years later, when the Beirut hostage, The Rev Terry Waite, landed there after he was released from his terrible imprisonment.

After spending the night at Lyneham, I started the next morning on the last stage of my final homecoming. My orders were to proceed to a Demobilisation Centre. My very first posting in the RAF was, as you have read, to a place that was just about as far away as you could get from my hometown in Blackpool. My final posting was - believe it or not - just about as near as you could get to Blackpool.

MAKE IT DO

1947 - The last of =the RAF

The Demobilisation Centre was at Warton between Lytham and Freckleton. I was issued with a suit, a shirt, shoes, socks, etc, and a trilby and a raincoat. I had no kit to hand, as all the officers' clothing belonged to Him and was not supplied by the RAF. I sold the suit sometime later. At the time of demobilisation, each service personnel was given a gratuity according to their final rank and the length of their service.

I had completed seven and a quarter years of service, and as one would expect of the grateful British Government, I was awarded the princely sum of one hundred and fourteen pounds. I was astounded and dismayed. Not only had I lost a fair sum of pay when I was commissioned as a Flight Sergeant, but I was also about to lose pay that had been deducted while I was a Prisoner of War. I had been away from home for a long time and had occasionally considered plans for the future.

So there you are, Peter and David - you have it—the war story.

Chapter 41

Closing Sortie

I realised upon my return to the UK that rationing of most commodities was still very much in place, and, of course, I was issued a Ration Book. Rationing continued until the mid-1950s - and even later for some items. I recall that in 1952, when I applied for a building licence in Southport, as wood was very much rationed, it was not an easy thing to obtain. The rules stated that a Building Licence could not be issued unless ownership of a plot of land could be proven, and one could not get a plot of land unless a Building Licence were already in place. This bureaucratic nonsense was resolved by a friendly and sensible builder agreeing to acknowledge that I was in possession of a plot that actually belonged to him. However, that problem was five years ahead, so let's go back to 1947.

It was late October 1947 when I left the RAF, and I had already decided that I could not face returning to the confines of a dreary Victorian Office. I realised that by quitting the Local Government Department, I was giving up several benefits, short working hours, good holidays, and a generous pension scheme. However, I would have to work for another forty years to achieve the pension, and that was a long time to commit to what would undoubtedly be a boring, clock-watching occupation. I, therefore, went down to see them and told them of my decision. So that was that. There is no need to write about my working life from then on, as you know it as well as I do.

There followed about four years of bachelor life, with memorable holidays around Europe, before, as a friend of mine remarked, "I noticed that you had started making nesting noises." Quite what they were, I do not know, but I understood the comment.

So, what did my time in the RAF teach me? Lots of things about life and people, but certain things were of great importance. That six years of talking and persuasion were far preferable to six days of war. Wars are awful and bring about awful deeds and miseries. There are no winners in the long run, but strangely, all the combatants are convinced that God is on their side. Peculiar - to say the least. But it is neither my job nor my wish here to discuss the stupidity of war. Therefore, I will limit my words to describe my postwar attitudes.

I had decided without any doubt about my ambitions in life. These were quite simple. A happy family, a nice house to live in, and hopefully, a car in the driveway were the things to aim for. Sufficient money to support a good but reasonable standard of living was great - a surfeit of money was non-essential. Most good things in life are free of purchasing power. Life as a Prisoner of War taught me this and other simple yet important things, such as being able to access water from a tap—and hot water as well—and having a warm, cosy place to live. Not being desperate for food, there are many others if you care to think about it for a few moments.

I had fortunately achieved my ambitions by the time I reached around forty. You may criticise me for being guilty of a lack of ambition if you wish - please yourself, but happiness often comes from being content with what you have, rather than what you are trying to achieve.

In 1949, an exceedingly pretty girl —perhaps I should say a very attractive young lady (both descriptions are correct)—came into my life, and we got married. The fact that we were of different branches of the same Christian Faith caused problems. Those who knew, or thought they knew, all about the consequences of a "mixed marriage" voiced their opinions. I include relations, friends, and officials of the Church in these dissenters. Although at times I felt very much alone, I was nevertheless convinced that each and every one of them would, in time, be proved wrong. And so they were - every single one of them.

We had a lovely week's honeymoon in Paris, except for the fact that I, not Betty, was sick on the aeroplane. So much for being a pilot! And so we started our married life, which, as I write these words today, is exactly forty-seven years old. We were one of four couples who were all married about the same time, and all four couples are still together. It's not an easy thing to accomplish these days, apparently, but as far as my two sons are concerned, they both seem to be off to a good start, and I can do no more than wish them a long and happy married life.

We returned to the top half of Mother's house, which had been partially converted into an apartment, but I had only been in residence for a couple of months when I was transferred to another job in Southport. We took an apartment and immediately started the process of becoming householders. We were extremely fortunate in our quest, and although we were short of money, at least we had started climbing the ladder.

We were blessed with two healthy and intelligent sons, and after twelve years in our new house, we moved back to Blackpool. The rest is well-known history. I had always had a burning desire for my sons to attend university and get a degree. Not only did they both achieve this high standard of education, but they also went one step further and earned two degrees each. All of which makes me extremely proud.

And so, I have come to the end of my writing. The war story, which forms the bulk of my memoirs, is one of a million war stories and not one in a million, so I was reluctant to begin it. I think I have mentioned before that it is as accurate an account as possible for me to provide, and at least I have tried to comply with your requests.

If, by chance, it is not entirely what you wanted, then I am afraid you have no option but to:

"MAKE IT DO"

The Post-War Life of Ken Cam

Ken Cam was an incredibly special man, son, brother, husband, and father. He had remarkably simple tastes and pleasures, was a devoted husband and family man, and was always interested in motorcars and the mechanics of them. He was a very stable person, suffered no ill effects from the mental strain of war, prison camp, and captivity, the Death March of January 1945, or shooting down other aircraft. He told me three things about war.

- There are no winners, as everyone loses too much.
- He mentally filed all the bad memories in an imaginary cabinet and closed it in his mind.
- He vowed that even if he had to steal, he would never go hungry or be cold again as long as he lived.

Dad could put his mind to anything and design, build, or fix it. He was skilled in carpentry and woodworking, and an exceptional mechanic; he had a vast array of tools in his beloved garage. He was always servicing the family vehicles and servicing cars for his friends. He was the Company Treasurer of a local company from 1964 to 1984, where he was highly respected by the owners, his peers, and his staff. At work, he was keen on staff involvement, hosting occasional parties, and organising various staff trips to foster camaraderie. He had few but remarkably close friends, and he loved vacationing in France, as he was very proficient in the French language and enjoyed chatting with the local French people.

He designed and built his refrigerator in the kitchen of our new house on Lynton Road in Southport, and I recall someone from a major appliance company visiting the house in the early 1960s to inspect it.

Ken building his own car

He could not afford to buy a motorcar in the early 1960s, as he was paying for the new house. So, he built his own car and a garage to house it. I remember, during the long daylight summer evenings when we small children had to be in bed by 7:30 p.m., looking out of my bedroom window, I could see him working on his car until dark. Neighbours who would often walk by would stop and ask him questions about the vehicle each night. I remember all too well the evening in August 1963, when a reporter from the Southport Visitor newspaper came to interview Dad about the completed Homemade Car, "The Camden." He took photos of us pointing at the engine and, in my case, polishing the hubcaps. Dad sold the car after only a year or so. It cost him £350 to build over eighteen months.

Moving to Blackpool in August 1964 was a big shock for us. From a new, modern, centrally heated home on a quiet cul-de-sac in Southport, we moved to a larger but very cold, dank, and very run-down 1938 fixer-upper property on a main road, with no heating other than fireplaces. The main exterior colour was "Shocking

Peter, Ken, David and Betty Cam

Pink." We stayed in that house for ten years until we acquired central heating, although that was nothing for Dad. He worked tirelessly on that house himself for many years to renovate it. We even built a vehicle "servicing pit" in the garage. We lived there until 1984, when Mum and Dad (Betty and Ken) sold the house, and Dad retired at the age of 63. They bought their beloved two-bedroom bungalow in Thornton-Cleveleys, a few miles away, with Dad's sister, Kathleen, living just around the corner.

In 1977, Dad returned to the crash site in Linosa. He was a major attraction, as apart from the Allied invasion in 1943, little else had happened on the island.

This gentleman in the photograph saw Dad crash land and was first on the scene to find Dad injured.

The Post-War Life of Ken Cam

Traditional Sunday dinner at Mum and Dad's house was the pinnacle of everyone's week. The food was delicious, and by the early nineties, the Cam family had grown to eleven of us. Sadly, for Mum and Dad, however, the younger son (Peter, the writer) had decided that he had had enough of England and, for the future benefit of his family, emigrated to Miami, Florida, in October 1996 to start a new life. Unfortunately, Sundays were never the same again for all the Cams.

Dad enjoyed a lifetime of remarkably good health. The odd bout of flu and heavy colds during the winter months would put him to bed for a few days, and he did experience extremely high fevers, but other than an extremely painful gallbladder attack in 1962, he never had health issues. In August 2008, Peter, Dora, Carolyne, Juliette, and Daniel came over from Florida, and we had a fabulous family reunion at David's house with Mum, Dad, David, Jin Ee, Edward, and Honor. Dad had eye trouble by then. We all wondered when, or if, there would be a future "Camfam Reunion" as the years rolled by. Sadly, it was not to be!

A 1996 "Camfam Reunion"

Early in 2009, Dad was diagnosed with a serious health issue; the dreaded word cancer entered our lives. Twelve months on, in February 2010, Dad's doctors decided that the planned surgery could not now occur as he most likely would not survive it. The advice he received was to enjoy the next eight to nine months before the inevitable. He took it!

The Post-War Life of Ken Cam

And so, Dad left us on Monday, November 14, 2010, at the age of eighty-nine and three months. He was as intelligent and alert as ever, right until the very end. His last words to me in person were, "Thank you for being my son, Peter." His best friend, Douglas (also a Spitfire pilot), whom he mentions several times in the book, outlived Dad by ten years and passed away shortly before his hundredth birthday.

I was fortunate to have my dad for my entire life, until I was fifty-two. When he left us, I felt nothing but a massive sense of relief and elation, as I did not want him to suffer any more than he had. He was not used to feeling ill or dealing with physical pain. He experienced enough "pain" of a different sort, loneliness, death fearing, and uncertainty between 1940 and 1945. He was exhausted due to his physical condition, and I wanted him to rest. He used to call me "Pete's", and he did so when I last spoke to him the evening before he died. As you have read in his book, he was not as lucky as my brother and myself. He missed his dad his entire life, from the age of ten, in 1932, and he mentions this on several occasions in the book. This loss was most pronounced during his wartime low points as a pilot facing death daily, and when, as a POW, he did not know if he would live or die, today, tomorrow, next week, or if he would ever get home to England. All this at the tender age of twenty-two to twenty-four!

What an amazing life he had. He was loved and respected by everyone he knew, including his family, friends, coworkers, and the owners of the companies for which he worked. Everyone, including his wonderful family doctor, who was there for him until the end.

The Post-War Life of Ken Cam

From Ken's original manuscript: revisiting the infamous gutter and cattle trains in Innsbruck

There are a few other things you should be aware of. Dad had a huge aura that you could feel in his presence. It could be very intimidating. My school friends and my brother's school friends were subjected to it, and it could be quite terrifying when he walked into the back room to see what we were doing when we were teenagers. I remember as a child that if he looked at you when you had done something wrong, it would be frightening, as you thought that you were about to die. Otherwise, his smile and hearty laugh could melt you. He was always very generous, loving, and true. He was a wonderful father to us.

Dad authored this book between 1997 and 1999, completing it on July 28, 1999. We have just added to it and explained areas that needed elaboration, more detail, and photos. When an article about the Linosa crash-landing and Dad's capture appeared in the local evening paper,

The Post-War Life of Ken Cam

"The Blackpool Gazette," local politician and MP Harold Elletson came to the house and spent an afternoon with Dad. He was deeply interested in the story, particularly his post-war exploits in Italy, Egypt, Palestine, and Transjordan.

He asked Dad a whole series of questions and then told him, "Ken, you didn't know it, but you were working for MI6." That made Dad's Day. Dr Elletson, who was educated at Eton and spoke fluent Russian, first ran for election in Burnley in 1987.

Ken's Gazette article, written after he completed his memoir

What we did not know when he visited was that Mr. Elletson (now deceased) was not only the MP for Blackpool North, but also ostensibly working undercover for MI6 with frequent trips to Eastern Europe. It is reported that Prime Minister John Major granted him "special permission to continue his undercover role." When asked about this, Mr. Elletson dismissed it as apparent "schoolboy chatter."

On a driving trip to southern England with my brother David (Circa 2009), they visited the Tangmere Military and Aviation Museum. It was closed for whatever reason. David explained that Dad flew Spitfires from Tangmere in 1942. WHAT?? He instantly became a celebrity; staff appeared from all over, asking him questions and giving him a VIP tour. When they came upon the Spitfires' display, Dad asked my brother, "Is that an AZ C?" Yes, it was. "That is the plane I flew from here all those years ago," he said, and everyone was elated. The photo is shown below.

Peter Cam
Miami, FL, USA
April 2025.

KEN CAM

LIFE AND WAR TIMELINE

1921
August:
Born in Blackpool, England.

1939
September:
Joins Blackpool LDV (Local Defense Volunteers)

1940
June:
Volunteers for the RAF (Royal Air Force) as a mechanic. Promoted to Pilot Under Training.

1941
December:
Posted to 234 Squadron at RAF Ibsley.

1942
May:
Posted to Portreath, Cornwall.

1942
September.
Posted to Digby, Lincolnshire to 242 Squadron. Sets sail for the Mediterranean the following month.

1942
November:
Arrives at Algiers in North Africa.

1943
Promoted to Flying Officer

1943
June:
Crash lands on Linosa Island and becomes POW.

1943
July:
Arrives in Taranto Harbour in a submarine.

1943
October/November:
Taken by train (including cattle truck trains) to Stalag Luft III Prison Camp in Sagan, Poland. Journey via Italy and Austria.

1945
January:
Begins what would later be known as the "Death March". POWs were marched west in freezing conditions, with little food or shelter.

1945
April:
Arrives in Lübeck via Hamburg before hitchhiking to Brussels.

1945
May:
Flies from Brussels to RAF Cosford in Shropshire before arriving home in Blackpool.

1946
Posted to RAF Amman in the Middle East.

1947
October:
Retires from RAF.

1977
Returns to Linosa to revisit crash site.

2010
November:
Ken Cam passes away.

Made in the USA
Columbia, SC
12 June 2025